T0012505

SWEDEN

THE ESSENTIAL GUIDE TO CUSTOMS & CULTURE

NEIL SHIPLEY

KUPERARD

"The real voyage of discovery consists not in seeking new landscapes, but in having new eyes."

Adapted from Marcel Proust, *Remembrance of Things Past*.

ISBN 978 1 78702 288 1
British Library Cataloguing in Publication Data
A CIP catalogue entry for this book is available
from the British Library

First published in Great Britain
by Kuperard, an imprint of Bravo Ltd
59 Hutton Grove, London N12 8DS
Tel: +44 (0) 20 8446 2440
www.culturesmart.co.uk
Inquiries: publicity@kuperard.co.uk

Design Bobby Birchall
Printed in Türkiye by Elma Basim

The Culture Smart! series is continuing to expand.
All Culture Smart! guides are available as e-books, and many
as audio books. For further information and latest titles visit
www.culturesmart.co.uk

NEIL SHIPLEY is an intercultural trainer and lecturer from Stockton-on-Tees in County Durham, England. He has a B.A. in Literature from the University of Essex, Colchester, and an M.A. in Intercultural Competence from Donau University in Austria. In 1994 he headed to Sweden, intending to live there for a year before moving on. Seduced by the beauty of the countryside, the coolness of the cities, and the values of the people, he stayed.

Today Neil is firmly rooted in Swedish society and is a leading expert on Swedish culture. He has lectured in more than fifty countries and has worked with many international organizations as well as the Swedish government, lecturing and providing seminars on Swedish culture and society. Since 2013 he has been writting a popular blog called "Watching the Swedes," where he shares his perspectives on Swedish life. Throughout his years in Sweden Neil has witnessed many changes. What remains unaltered is his long-lasting attachment to this cool country in the North.

CONTENTS

INTRODUCTION

The Culture Smart! guides begin where most other travel books end. They emphasize people, not places. Written for the inquiring traveler who wants more than research into hotels, sight-seeing, and transportation, they offer an insight into the human dimension of a country, based on the values and attitudes of its people.

Sweden is, in many senses, an unspoiled paradise of achingly beautiful archipelagos, forests, mountains, lakes, and coastlines. This surprisingly varied countryside is full of contrasts and contradictions—as is its population.

If you are visiting Sweden for more than a few days, you will get much more out of your trip if you have a good background in the beliefs that make up the foundation of the Swedish way of life. *Culture Smart! Sweden* will help you to go beyond the polite phase, so that you gain a greater understanding of what is important to the Swedes and why they act the way they do. It considers the influence of Sweden's geography and history in shaping the national character. There is vital information on deep-rooted Swedish values and attitudes, and a comprehensive overview of doing business in Sweden—essential for anyone who needs to understand the unique way that Swedish businesses operate.

As for socializing, you will get an insider's perspective on visiting a Swedish home, and on the qualities that Swedes most appreciate in a guest. With detailed chapters on the customs and traditions that form the cornerstones of Swedish life, and information on where and how to meet and communicate with Swedes, this book is an indispensable guide to the "real" Sweden.

Swedish society is based on the belief in equality, independence, self-expression, and respect. It is very rights-driven, with a strong commitment to maintaining a safe and secure "home of the people." The Swedes are justifiably proud of many aspects of the egalitarian society they have created, which provides basic healthcare, education, and social welfare benefits for all.

Although historically strongly Lutheran, the Swedes today are a largely secular people who make life decisions from a non-religious, logical standpoint. This does not, however, mean that they are not spiritual. It is in the natural environment that many Swedes find spiritual fulfillment—in the forests, on the lakes, and in the mountains. For many Swedes, reverence for nature is a kind of religion.

Culture Smart! Sweden provides a cultural roadmap to use in navigating the new social and professional situations you will encounter as a visitor. It aims to help you to build good business relationships and make firm friends with the welcoming and fair-minded people who live and work here.

Have a great trip!

Official Name	Kingdom of Sweden (Kungariket Sverige)	
Capital City	Stockholm	Pop. 2,210,000 (metropolitan area)
Main Cities	Göteborg (Gothenburg), Malmö, Uppsala, Västerås, Örebro, Linköping	
Area	204,034.5 sq. miles (528,447 sq. km): 63% forest; 9% lakes and rivers; 7% farming; 3% built-on; 8% marshland; 3% mountain and rock; 7% other	
Climate	Temperate and varied	
Currency	Swedish krona (pl. kronor). In English, Crown. In 2023, 1 USD = SEK 10.3; 1 Euro = SEK11.4; 1 GBP = SEK 12.9. Sweden is not part of the Eurozone.	
Population	10.4 million. Approx. 50/50 women/men	Average life expectancy: 81 for men and 85 for women
Ethnic Makeup	Approx. 75% Swedes; approx. 25% with "foreign background" (most common origins: Finland, Iraq, Syria, Iran, Somalia, Bosnia)	"Foreign background" incls. people with parents born outside Sweden (even if they were born in Sweden). The Sámi (Lapps) are the indigenous people (approx. 20,000).
Family Makeup	30% married; average 1.7 children per family	
Language	Swedish. Official minority langs.: Finnish, Sámi, Romani, Yiddish, and Meänkieli (spoken in the Tornedal region). All adults and many children are fluent in English.	
Religion	Church and State separated. Approx. 80% are atheist or agnostic. The main religion is Christianity: Lutheran Church of Sweden. Other denominations incl. Pentecostal, Catholic, and independent churches. Second-largest religion is Islam. Others incl. Eastern Orthodox, Judaism, Buddhism, and Hinduism.	

Government	Constitutional monarchy, parliamentary democracy. The monarch has no political power.	Parliament, the Riksdag, has 349 members, elected every four years. In 2020 there was almost 50/50 representation of men/women.
Media	Swedish Broadcasting Corporation runs two public service channels, SVT1 and SVT2, as well as Radio Sweden and the streaming site SVT Play. The largest commercial channel is TV4, which also streams on TV4 Play. Many digital channels. Scheduled TV is in decline in favor of streaming sites.	
Press	Main broadsheet and digital newspapers are *Dagens Nyheter* and *Svenska Dagbladet*. Popular regional papers incl.*Göteborgs Posten*, *Sydsvenska Dagbladet*. Tabloids such as *Expressen* and *Aftonbladet* also exist in paper and digital formats. Approx. 62% read the news digitally. Sales for both printed and digital news sources are declining.	
Social Media	Approx. 80% of Swedes use Facebook and 70% use Instagram. Other platforms are YouTube, Snapchat, and Twitter.	82% use streaming sites such as Netflix, HBO, Amazon Prime, ViaSat, and C-More.
Electricity	220 volts, 50 Hz.	Plugs are two-pronged. Adapters required, esp. for visitors from outside the EU.
Internet Domain	.se	
Telephone	Sweden's country code is 46. To call within Sweden, dial 0 + the city code + the local number.	WhatsApp, Facetime, Skype, and Messenger are widely used.

CHAPTER ONE

LAND & PEOPLE

When you think of Sweden, what comes to mind? Perhaps performance artists such as ABBA, Zara Larsson, Robyn, or Roxette; or sportspeople like Zlatan Ibrahimović, Björn Borg, or Henrik Stenson? You may think of marauding Vikings, the classic *smorgasbord*, Absolut Vodka, or Swedish massage; or international brands such as Ikea, Volvo, and H&M. Or do images of green forests, cold lakes, rocky coastlines, and snowy mountains with bracing fresh air float to the fore?

This variety of associations sums Sweden up very well. Sweden might be a sparsely populated land in the far north of Europe, but it is a country that has made an impact. From the Vikings to the merchants, the tourists, and the entrepreneurs, Swedes have always had a drive to venture beyond their borders to the world outside. Today Sweden is a truly international country with a global reach, but two hundred years ago its focus was on conquering and controlling the neighboring regions around the Baltic Sea.

Aerial view from the top of the Kebnekaise Mountain.

GEOGRAPHICAL SNAPSHOT

Sweden is a long, narrow country in the center of
Scandinavia, with Norway to its west and Finland to
the east. In the north, it is spectacular and mountainous,
and its largest mountain, Kebnekaise, is 93 miles (150 km)
north of the Arctic Circle and towers 6,880 feet (2,097 m)
above sea level. The glaciated southern peak used to
be higher but has shrunk by about 7.8 feet (roughly
24 m) during the last fifty years. To the south, Sweden is
connected to Denmark and the European continent by the
large and impressive Öresund Bridge. Fans of the Nordic
noir series "The Bridge" may recognize it as the grisly
location of a corpse found at midpoint, half in Sweden
and half in Denmark.

The southern tip of Sweden is characterized by open
rolling countryside and long, sandy beaches. This type

The skerry island of Romsoe in the western Swedish archipelago.

of geography is unusual for Sweden, which is mostly covered with dense pine, spruce, and fir forests. Of Sweden's 204,034.53 square miles (528,447 sq km), 63 percent is forested, and less than 10 percent is cultivated.

Sweden is a land of water: a long coastal perimeter, stunning archipelagos, wild rivers, canals, and serene lakes. It has two breathtaking archipelagos—to the west in the North Sea and in the eastern Baltic Sea. The archipelago off the east coast has more than 25,000 islands of varying size, ranging from barren, uninhabited skerries to larger residential islands with rocky coastlines. In the Baltic Sea, Sweden has two large, populated islands—Öland and Gotland.

Of the thousands of lakes in Sweden, lakes Vättern and Vänern are two of the largest in Europe. The Göta Canal, with its many locks, connects these lakes and

joins Stockholm on the east coast with Gothenburg on the west. This has earned it the name Sweden's "Blue Ribbon."

Most of the population live in the southern half of the country in the major urban regions of Stockholm, Gothenburg, and Malmö. In the far north of the country, in a geographical area covering Sweden, Norway, Russia, and Finland, live Sweden's indigenous population—the Sámi. The largest population of Sámi lives in Norway, and in Sweden there are currently around 20,000. Approximately 10 percent survive to this day on breeding reindeer. Sweden's most northerly town, Kiruna, is situated above the Arctic Circle and has a population of approximately 17,000.

Rural idyll as Sweden's brief fall gives way to the onset of winter.

CLIMATE

The Swedish climate is varied. Winters are long, dark, and often cold, which is why most Swedes welcome the arrival of the snow to lighten up the surroundings. Depending on location, snow can remain on the ground until any time between November and May. To combat the winter blues, the Swedes spend as much time as possible outdoors in the daylight, or participate in winter sports such as skating on the frozen lakes. Winter travel to tropical climes is also very popular.

In the far north, winter can mean twenty-four hours of darkness, while the summer offers the same amount of daylight. Temperatures vary depending on location.

APPROXIMATE AVERAGE TEMPERATURES

	January	July
Malmö	32°F / 0°C	68°F/ 20°C
Stockholm	30°F/ -1 °C	70°F/ 21°C
Kiruna	7°F / -14.0°C	55.5°F/ 13°C

AVERAGE DAYLIGHT

	January	July
Malmö	7 hours	17 hours
Stockholm	6 hours	18 hours
Kiruna	0 hours	24 hours

Many visitors experience a difference in the Swedes depending on if they visit in the summer or the winter. This has a lot to do with the weather. In summer, you may be greeted by an open, outgoing population who fill the parks, lakes, and cafés with a lively buzz. In winter, however, the Swedes tend to be more closed and introverted, rushing from one appointment to another to avoid the worst of the weather and staying at home in front of the television.

Spring and fall are distinct but short, and many Swedes live by the motto *carpe diem*—if the day looks promising in terms of sun, they drop everything and seize the opportunity to go outdoors. This urge is often incomprehensible to people coming from more stable and predictable climates.

THE SWEDISH PEOPLE: A BRIEF HISTORY

The Viking Age (800–1050 CE)

In the ninth century Scandinavia—modern Denmark, Norway, and Sweden—was inhabited by a loose grouping of warlike Teutonic tribes known as the Vikings.

The Vikings raided most of Europe from the sea, gaining a fearsome reputation for brutality and destructiveness. The Danish and Norwegian Vikings took to the seas heading west and south, toward Ireland, Iceland, England, and France: the Swedish Vikings sailed mainly east, raiding and settling along the rivers of Russia, and reaching as far as Baghdad and Constantinople, which they called Miklagård. Excellent shipbuilders, they developed flat-bottomed long boats, enabling them to sail swiftly in and around the many islands and across lakes, and to carry the boats over dry land when necessary. Many of their conquests were due to this surprise factor.

Viking reenactment at Läckö castle in Västra Götaland.

Although in theory the boats would have allowed the Vikings to establish trade with other parts of the world, to begin with they found it more expedient to raid, plunder, and take slaves. Each warrior was entitled to his fair share of the spoils, a practice that we see reflected in the value system of Swedish citizens today.

The Vikings had a kind of parliament called a *Thing*, where issues were collectively discussed and resolved. There was no hereditary leadership—chiefs were mostly elected on merit—and women could own property, request a divorce, and reclaim their dowries if their marriages ended.

From the Dark Ages to Enlightenment

The Viking conquests were not all purely destructive. In time, as merchants and settlers, they also interacted peaceably with other peoples, to their mutual benefit. In 1000 CE Sweden embraced Christianity and was transformed into a land of medieval kings supported by taxation. By 1210 an alliance was formed between Church and State, which was only officially dissolved in 2000.

Concurrent with the acceptance of Christianity was the emergence of an aristocracy; rival dynasties competed for control of the Swedish kingdom, and a series of crusades incorporated western Finland. Dynastic struggles within all three Scandinavian countries led to the passing of the Swedish crown to Denmark, whose Queen Margareta became the most powerful ruler Scandinavia had ever known. Her political maneuverings resulted in the 1397 Union of Kalmar, which united

Sweden, Norway, and Denmark. Thereafter Sweden was effectively ruled by a succession of regents.

The Union was plagued for more than a hundred years by conflict and revolt. The era came to an end in 1520 when the Danish King Christian II hosted a banquet in Stockholm as a peace overture and then, at its conclusion, locked the doors and beheaded more than eighty Swedish noblemen whom he considered disloyal. This

St. Bridget of Sweden, from the altarpiece in Salem Church, Södermanland.

incident is known as the "Stockholm Bloodbath" and in Sweden the king is remembered as "Christian the Tyrant."

The Vasas

Unlike his father, brothers, and brother-in-law, Gustav Vasa survived the "Stockholm Bloodbath" to lead an uprising. He is said to have escaped on cross-country skis across Sweden to enlist the aid of those living in the province of Dalarna and in Norway. The reenactment of this feat is seen today in the famous *Vasaloppet*, or Vasa ski marathon, the world's longest cross-country skiing competition.

Gustav Vasa, c.1550.

Gustav Vasa was crowned King of Sweden on June 6, 1523, and the Kalmar Union came to an end. The Swedes today celebrate June 6 as their national day.

Under Gustav Vasa, Sweden was transformed into a nation based on a tiered class system of nobility, clergy, merchants, and peasants. Each of these "four estates" was represented in the Riksdag (parliament), convening and voting separately, and decisions were carried by a three to one estates majority. This system endured until 1865.

A powerful, enlightened, but ruthless ruler, Gustav Vasa solved the country's financial crisis by transferring all Church property to the Crown in 1527, initiating the Swedish Reformation. Eventually Lutheranism came to replace Roman Catholicism as the state religion. In 1544 he established a hereditary monarchy. Lutheranism and the hereditary monarchy survive to this day.

The Swedish Empire

From 1611 to 1721 Sweden was the dominant power in northern Europe, exercising territorial control over much of the Baltic region. During this 110-year period the country was at war for seventy-two years, notably entering Europe's Thirty Years War (1618–48) in 1631 against the

Habsburg rulers of the Holy Roman Empire. The military brilliance of Gustav II Adolf (1611–32), "the Lion of the North," saved Protestantism in Germany. He made Stockholm Sweden's administrative capital.

His daughter Kristina (1633–54) became Sweden's first female monarch at the age of six. Her reluctance to marry caused the throne to be passed on to her cousin Karl Gustav. She abdicated and converted to Catholicism and is buried in the Vatican. As a result of the scandal, the laws of succession were changed, barring women from the throne. They were repealed in 1980, paving the way for Sweden's current heir apparent, Crown Princess Victoria, to succeed to the throne.

Gustav II Adolf at the Battle of Breitenfeld, 1631, by Johann Walter.

The Carolean Era

King Karl X Gustav (1654–60) conquered Poland, invaded Denmark in a surprise move by leading his army across the frozen sea, and secured the southern Sweden provinces. Karl XI (1660–97) divided the land more evenly between the Crown, the nobility, and the peasants, while accruing absolute power. Karl XII (1697–1718) came to power as a teenager. His reign was controversial because he was always waging war. In 1718, he was shot in the head while besieging a fortress in Norway. By this time, he had lost almost all the territories Sweden had gained, with the exception of Finland and a small portion of Poland. Of the three treaties signed at this time, the most important was that signed in 1721 with Russia. It established certain present-day boundaries with Finland and Russia, and ended 150 years of nearly continuous war. A statue of this warmongering king stands in Stockholm's Kungsträdgården park—his arm raised and pointing to Russia.

The Age of Liberty and the Gustavian Era

The eighteenth century was known as Sweden's "Age of Liberty." In 1719, a new constitution was adopted, transferring political power from the king to parliament (the Riksdag), which was dominated by the nobles. This parliamentary rule lasted until around 1770. In 1772, the new king, Gustav III, staged a bloodless coup and claimed absolute power for himself.

An enlightened despot, Gustav III presided over a golden age in Swedish culture. He built the Royal Opera House and the Royal Dramatic Theater in Stockholm, and established the exquisite theater at Drottningholm Palace. In 1786, he founded the Swedish Academy, which today awards the Nobel Prize for Literature. However, he antagonized the nobility by attacking their privileges. In 1792, he was assassinated at a masked ball at the Opera.

His son, Gustaf IV Adolf, abdicated and fled Sweden after losing Finland to Russia in the Napoleonic Wars in 1809. This cost Sweden one third of its land and marked the end of an era.

The Bernadottes

The nineteenth century again saw power shifting from the Crown to the people. Lacking an heir to the throne, the nobles of the restored Riksdag offered Napoleon's marshal, Count Jean-Baptiste Bernadotte, the position of Crown Prince of Sweden. He was crowned in 1810 and is the ancestor of the current royal family who bear the same surname. A new constitution was adopted that removed the absolute power of the monarch and diminished the privileges of the aristocracy, dividing power between the king, the government, and parliament.

In 1812 Bernadotte allied Sweden with Russia against France. In 1813 he defeated his former commander, Napoleon, in the Battle of Leipzig, and then attacked Denmark, forcing it to sign the Treaty of Kiel in 1814, ceding Norway to Sweden. This was the last war Sweden participated in. The union between Norway and Sweden lasted nearly one hundred years, from 1814 to 1905. Bernadotte ruled Sweden from 1818 to 1844 as Karl XIV Johan.

During this century of peace the Swedish population exploded. Given the shortage of arable land, this put a huge strain on the largely agricultural economy, and crop failure led to famine and economic hardship. Between 1850 and 1930, 1.5 million people emigrated, mostly to the United States, to find a better life. Some also longed for greater religious freedom. The classic Swedish novel series *The Emigrants* by Vilhelm Moberg depicts this era in Swedish history, as does the musical *Kristina from Duvemåla.*

The Swedish Industrial Revolution

Sweden's Industrial Revolution began toward the end of the 1800s and by 1900 the population had grown to 5 million. Growing numbers migrated to the towns to work in industry, since the land could no longer support them.

Free enterprise was established with the abolition of trade guilds and monopolies in 1846. This era was significant for political reform: a bicameral legislature was created, neutrality was adopted in foreign affairs, and in 1905 the union with Norway was dissolved. The year 1907 saw the adoption of proportional representation and universal suffrage.

These values are seen today in the platform of the Social Democratic party, founded in 1889. It has been the dominant political party in Sweden since 1932, with a few periods of exceptions. This consistency of government has contributed significantly to the country's stability over the past seventy years.

The Welfare State
In 1936 the Social Democrats and the Agrarian Party developed the concept of a Welfare State that would guarantee unemployment benefits, paid holidays, childcare, and the right to good housing. This was perfected by the Social Democrats from 1947 to 1969. The result of this "cradle to grave" safety net was that poverty virtually disappeared in Sweden for a period. Today, the Welfare State has been somewhat dismantled and privatized in line with a growing population, changing social attitudes, and the introduction of more market-driven policies.

Nonalignment
During the First and Second World Wars Sweden's policy of nonalignment and neutrality helped to preserve the country's economy. Sweden's role during the Second World War has been the subject of much debate, with its neutrality being questioned. It traded with both sides, selling iron. In 1940–43, under duress, it permitted limited transit of German forces through its territory toward Norway. Covert assistance was also given to the Allies.

The Postwar Years
After the war, having avoided conflict and invasion, Sweden was in a strong economic position and the

policy of non-alignment continued, including a rejection of NATO membership. For twenty-three years the country had the same prime minister, Tage Elander, who presided over a stable period of unprecedented prosperity. As more people moved to the cities, a huge housing shortage occurred. Between 1965 and 1974 the government started the "Million Project"—to build a million homes to house the growing population. Most of these properties exist today and, while many are renovated, some are crumbling.

This period also marked the genesis of mass immigration to Sweden, initially from southern Europe, and then from Chile, Iran, and the Balkan region. In 1974 a constitutional change removed the remaining political powers of the monarch, and in 1995 Sweden joined the European Union. Sweden has held the EU presidency twice—in 2001 and 2009. Three violent deaths—the assassination of Prime Minister Olof Palme in 1986, the murder of Foreign Minister Anna Lindh in 2003, and the devastating terrorist attack on Sweden's main shopping street in 2017—have caused the Swedes to reassess their self-perception as a model, nonviolent society.

Another tragedy to shock Sweden occurred on Wednesday, September 28, 1994. The cruise ship *Estonia*, carrying 989 people, was crossing the Baltic Sea, *en route* from Tallinn, Estonia, to Stockholm when she sank: 852 people died that day, of whom 504 were Swedes.

The spectacular cable-stayed Öresund Bridge provides road and rail links to Denmark.

The New Millenium

On July 1, 2000, a momentous event occurred in Sweden. With the opening of the Öresund Bridge connecting Sweden to Denmark, Sweden became connected to the Continent in a way that had never previously been possible. This opened up the entire Malmö–Copenhagen area to become one of Scandinavia's most prosperous regions.

In 2003, despite being a strong supporter of the EU, Sweden neverless decided to not adopt the Euro as the country's official currency. In 2006, the Social Democrats lost the national elections and the conservative Moderate Party emerged as the main victor. Together with the Center Party, the Liberal Party, and the Christian Democrats, it formed a center-right coalition government called The Alliance, headed by Prime Minister Fredrik Reinfeldt. It stayed in power until 2014 and during its two terms of office introduced a series of significant political and social changes, such as liberalized terms of employment, reduced taxes, and reduced benefits for the sick and the unemployed.

In 2004, 20,000 Swedes were on holiday in Thailand and Southeast Asia when the tsunami struck land. With 543 deaths, Sweden was the most affected country in Europe, and the ripple effect of this is still being felt today. In 2009, gender-neutral marriage was legalized in Sweden, and in 2010 a far-right party entered the parliament for the first time. During the second decade of the twenty-first century Swedish politics became even more polarized, reflecting deepening divisions in society.

The Social Democrats regained power in 2014 and, together with the Greens, formed a minority coalition. In 2018, the results of the general elections were so inconclusive that it took around five months to form a government—consisting of the Social Democrats and the Greens, with the Left Party, the Liberals, and the Center Party lending their support.

In 2020, due to instability in the Baltic and Russia's border regions, the Swedish parliament voted for an increase in military spending. Stockholm significantly reinforced its defenses on the Swedish island of Gotland. Against the government's will, there was also a majority vote in parliament to consider joining NATO—in direct contradiction of the country's long-held principle of military nonalignment.

THE SWEDES TODAY

For a small country, Sweden has done a great job in promoting itself abroad. It almost always appears in the top five of global surveys on quality of life, opportunity, entrepreneurship, and equality. This means that Sweden is generally perceived as a fair, progressive, and modern country. Foreign critics, however, claim that it is now an unstable society, usually with reference to the impact of immigration or to Sweden's controversially mild handling of the coronavirus pandemic in 2020.

Sweden has gone from being a relatively homogeneous society to a multicultural one in less than a century. Today, about 25 percent of its population of 10.4 million is categorized as having a foreign background, giving Sweden the highest proportion of immigrants of all the Nordic countries. Many immigrants are refugees, although there is also a large proportion of migrants moving to Sweden for professional work purposes. The military conflict in Syria created chaos in Europe, with a wave of millions of refugees arriving on Mediterranean shores. Sweden received approximately 300,000 asylum seekers in 2015–16, one of the largest per-capita intakes in the EU. This caused lasting rifts in Swedish society, with some Swedes demanding a total freeze on immigration. Others, proud of the country's humanitarian approach, welcomed the new arrivals. However, in recent years, stricter immigration laws have been put in place to control the influx and make integration more manageable.

THE SÁMI POPULATION

Sweden's indigenous people are the Sámi. Their homeland is called Sápmi and covers a wide area north of the Arctic Circle within Norway, Sweden, Russia, and Finland. There is currently no call for a sovereign state, but the Sámi do petition for greater autonomy in their respective countries. Today, there are an estimated 20,000 Sámis in Sweden who support themselves in a variety of ways, including fishing and reindeer husbandry. After a history of oppression and injustice, in which they were subjected to eugenic research, discrimination, and land right disputes, in 1989 Sweden finally recognized the existence of the "Sámi nation." In 1993, the Swedish Sámi Parliament was inaugurated, and Sámi children were allowed to be taught in their native language. Since 2010, Laponiatjuottjudus, a local administrative organization with Sámi majority control, has governed the UNESCO World Heritage Site of Laponia.

In 1998, Sweden formally apologized for the wrongs committed against the Sámi. The Sámi languages are recognized by Swedish law as official national minority languages. In 2016, the film *Sámi Blood* was released to critical acclaim. Set in the 1930s, it addressed this shameful part of history in Sweden.

SWEDEN'S CITIES

Sweden's cities are not large by international standards, but that is what makes them charming. There are three

View of Stockholm's old town (Gamla Stan) from the top of City Hall.

major cities and urban areas: Stockholm, Gothenburg, and Malmö. The capital city of Stockholm is often called "the Venice of the North." Built on fourteen islands, it looks out onto another 25,000 islands in the Swedish archipelago. With a metropolitan population of around 2,210,000, it is the largest city in Sweden. It's expansion is reflected in continuous construction work—new motorways, new housing areas, and new subway lines. One enormous project, the Slussen project, started in 2015, aimed to prevent a dilapidated traffic hub in the center of Stockholm from sinking into the sea. A major engineering feat and a key part of the project, "the Golden Bridge," linking the south of Stockholm to the Old Town, was inaugurated by the Swedish king in October 2020. Slightly to the north of Stockholm is the university town of Uppsala (population 230,000) with its magnificent, eight-hundred-year-old cathedral.

The urban landscape of Malmö.

Gothenburg (Göteborg, population 995,000) dominates Sweden's west coast and is a major gateway for commercial shipping and cruise ships. Known for its friendly welcome, Gothenburg faces out toward an archipelago and the often blustery North Sea. There is an affectionate rivalry between those living in predominantly blue-collar Gothenburg and the "*noll–åttas*" (0–8s), a pejorative term for Stockholmers, derived from the city code of their telephone numbers.

At the southern tip of Sweden, in the county of Skåne, lies Malmö (population 643,000). This is Sweden's third-largest city, located opposite Copenhagen and an integral part of the growing Öresund region, where more than 4,000,000 live on both sides of the water. On the seafront is Malmö's signature building, Turning Torso. Opened in 2005, this is a neo-futurist residential tower, the first twisted skyscraper in the world, and the tallest building in Scandinavia.

With Copenhagen only a twenty-minute train ride from Malmö over the Öresund Bridge, it is not surprising that local residents look to the Danish capital for influence rather than to Stockholm, which can feel somewhat remote to them. People can also make the crossing on ferries from neighboring Helsingborg to the Danish town of Helsingör, where Hamlet's fictional castle is located. The university city of Lund (population 100,000) is only 19 miles (30 km) away, and was at one time the religious capital of an extensive territory controlled by the Catholic Church that stretched from Iceland to Finland. Otherwise, much of urban Sweden comprises a few small cities and many smaller towns.

GOVERNMENT

Sweden is a parliamentary democracy, with all power stemming from the people. Elections are held on the second Sunday of September every four years, usually with a very high turnout. The unicameral parliament, the Riksdag, has 349 members, and seats are distributed according to proportional representation. As a consequence, governments tend to be multiparty coalitions. In order to minimize the number of parties in parliament, however, there is one exception to the rule of full representation—a party must receive at least 4 percent of all votes cast in the election to qualify for seats.

THE MAIN PARTIES

In 2021 there were eight parties in the Swedish parliament.

Socialdemokraterna (Social Democrats): Left–center party. Traditionally, believed that the public sector should control social services, although this has shifted in recent years to align with changing public opinion. Pro-labor unions, it attracts around 25 percent of the total vote.

Moderaterna (Moderates): Right-wing, conservative. Believe in lower taxes and a market economy based on free competition, including privatization of social services. Attracts around 20 percent of the total vote.

Sverigedemokraterna (Swedish Democrats): Right-wing, nationalistic party. Has a conservative and traditional viewpoint on family and social policies. Main political platform is the restriction of immigration and the preservation of Swedish culture. First entering parliament in 2010, it has grown rapidly in popularity to around 18 percent of the vote.

Liberalerna (Liberals): Exact center. Lies between the Moderates and the Social Democrats and swings from one to the other. Platform: "social responsibility without socialism." Education is the main issue. Usually attracts less than 10 percent of the vote.

Kristdemokraterna (Christian Democrats): Right-wing with conservative family-oriented policies profiling crime and punishment. Attracts 5–10 percent of the vote.

Vänsterpartiet (Left Party): The most left-wing. Believes in a state-owned economy and public services such as health care. Attracts around 10 percent of the vote.

Centern (Center Party): Profiled as a non left-wing environmental party with close ties to rural Sweden. Attracts between 5–10 percent of the vote.

Miljöpartiet (Green Party): Green. Environmental issues and climate change are the focal points. Attracts mostly young people with a left-wing orientation. Often allied with the Social Democrats and therefore part of a red–green coalition government. Attracts between 5–10 percent of the vote.

An additional party is the **Feministiska Initiativet (Feminist Initiative).** Not represented in the parliament as they are under the 4 percent entrance bar. Focused on anti-racist feminism, they want to renew the political system to arrive at a more equal society for all its citizens.

CHAPTER TWO

VALUES & ATTITUDES

The Swedes are, of course, as diverse as any other people and you will find all types in Swedish society. Despite differences between individuals, however, there is definitely a national "brand," consisting of values that the country promotes outside its borders and which families and schools reinforce among their children. Swedish values are based strongly on the belief in equality, independence, self-expression, and respect. Most Swedish people are very rights-driven and open. Although the unquestioning social solidarity of former times may have diminished, they still aspire to honesty, harmony, and lack of confrontation in their private lives.

Socially, the Swedes tend to be more reserved and less expressive than people from other countries, but scratch the surface and you will find a dry sense of humor, an affinity with nature, and a great love of home and family.

UNQUESTIONABLE EQUALITY

A strong driving value in Sweden is equality, which is enshrined in law. This value is embedded throughout society, in politics, work practices, and family life. Sweden has spent decades working on equal rights policies and legislation, and has produced many internationally recognized human rights advocates—Dag Hammarskjöld, Alva Myrdal, and Raoul Wallenberg, to mention a few.

Gender Equality
In 1842, girls were legally permitted to go to school, and in 1919 women received the right to vote. In 1938, birth control and abortion on medical, humanitarian, or eugenical grounds were legalized. Although equality between the genders has come far in Sweden, some argue that there is still a way to go. Since 1980, gender discrimination has been illegal in Sweden, but women are not as well represented as men in higher managerial positions and the gender pay gap is the subject of an ongoing debate. Certain structures have been put in place to protect women and to help them avoid falling into the "women's trap" (when a woman, for economic reasons, is forced to stay home to look after children and thereby misses out on opportunities in the workplace). For example, paid parental leave is granted, and jobs are secure. Today, parental leave is often shared between the parents, with three months earmarked for each parent. The three months known as "pappa months" encourage

fathers to stay at home so that women can go to work. Parents are provided with a state benefit equivalent to 80 percent of their salary, up to a cap. Today Sweden has an Equality Ombudsman and a Minister of Gender Equality.

Children's Rights

In Sweden, it is undeniable that the concept of equality extends to children. This is a distinctive part of Swedish parenting techniques, where children are often involved in decisions that affect them. Swedish parents will also tend to speak calmly and rationally to misbehaving children. Rarely will you see a parent yell at their child in anger. In 1979, Sweden was the first country in the

Getting around town. Mother and child in Örebro, central Sweden.

world to prohibit corporate punishment of children and it was one of the first nations to ratify the United Nations Convention on the Rights of the Child. Sweden also has an Ombudsman for Children, a government agency that represents their rights and interests. State-subsidized kindergarten is a right for all children and enables parents to go back to work without having to pay for expensive childcare.

Racial Equality

Education, health care, and social services are provided equally to all Swedes regardless of ethnicity or origin. The amended Discrimination Act of 2011 makes it illegal in Sweden to discriminate based on ethnicity, sex, transgender identity or expression, religion or other belief, disability, sexual orientation, or age. This, of course, does not mean that racial equality exists everywhere in Sweden. In 2019, the government launched a National Plan to combat racism, hate crime, online xenophobia, and intolerance. Despite this, the Swedish security service identifies a growing xenophobic and radical nationalist current. The most common types of racism are Islamophobia, antisemitism, and Afrophobia.

But there is a pushback—the Black Lives Matter movement of 2020 attracted hundreds of thousands of supporters protesting against systematic and daily racism in Sweden. In such a diverse society, with a growing political left–right divide, the issue of racial equality is a challenge likely to face generations to come.

LGBTQA Equality

Sweden has come a long way in legislating for the rights of LGBTQA people, including adoption rights (2003) and gender-neutral marriage (2009). Although in 1972 Sweden became the first country in the world to legally allow gender reassignment, it included mandatory sterilization— a clause that was lifted in 2013. It is largely within the transgender community that there is the greatest need for further work on equality, as transgender people still face intolerance and discrimination. (See page 57.)

The "*Du*" Reform

In modern Swedish, when you want to say "you" the word is "*du*." However, this was not always the case. Previously, it was considered more polite to address each other with the formal word for "you"—"*ni*"—or alternatively in the third person (he/she, *han/hon*), or as Mr./Mrs./Ms. (*herr, fru,* or *fröken*). The form of address used was a way to indicate status and subordination. This intrinsic inequality in the language was changed in the late 1960s in the "Du Reform," and today everybody says "*du*" regardless of their position in society, unless talking to a member of the royal family. The word "*ni*" still exists in Swedish and is used today as a plural form of "you."

FIERCE INDEPENDENCE

Swedish society encourages all people to be independent and self-supporting. Everybody is expected to take care of themselves, but to contribute with tax to support those who are not able to. Because of their strong sense of self-sufficiency, most Swedes have a high level of personal integrity and a need to be left alone, so they will be careful about interfering in each other's business. Help may not be offered, the consensus being that if you need help you will ask for it. Some people claim that this has led to an epidemic of loneliness in Swedish society. The 2016 documentary *The Swedish Theory of Love* explores this idea.

SELF EXPRESSION

Swedes believe strongly in the right to express themselves. Children are taught at an early age that they have the right to their opinion. This does not, however, mean that everybody always speaks their mind. Along with self-sufficiency and self-expression comes "self-actualization." Most Swedes believe they are in control of their own lives, they have the right to be who they want to be, love who they want to love, and live how they want to live. Due to conformist tendencies in society, this might not always be the case in practice—but it exists there as a fundamental value.

MUTUAL RESPECT AND PUNCTUALITY

Connected to independence and self-expression is the value of respect. As everybody is considered equal, their privacy, their opinions, and their choices should be respected. Not acknowledging this is a definite social *faux pas*, and many Swedes will easily apply the word "*kränkt*" (meaning violated, wronged) if they feel they have not been respected or that their rights have been infringed.

Most Swedes value punctuality and, although lateness is not a serious breach of respect, would regard it as discourteous. In private life, the Swedish concept of the "academic quarter" says it is socially acceptable to be fifteen minutes late. Being early, however, is avoided, with most people loitering outside until it is time to ring the doorbell.

In a business context, punctuality is a manifestation of the value of equality—everyone's time is equally important.

LAGOM: "JUST ENOUGH"

The Swedish word *lagom* has no equivalent in English but the concept is said to describe the basis of the Swedish national psyche. The closest translations are "just enough," "in moderation," or "sufficient." *Lagom* does not suggest that something is lacking, but rather has the connotation of appropriateness. *Lagom* is manifest throughout Swedish society—for example in the welfare state, where everybody receives enough, but not more than they need. Socially, it can explain certain interactions—for example, the giving of presents ideally

should not be over the top and showy, but instead *lagom*.
In 2017, the concept became hyped in the UK and USA
as a "Scandi-trend" and was described as a sustainable
substitute for over-consumerism. *Lagom* is a tricky
concept to grasp because it is subjective. *Lagom* for one
person is not necessarily *lagom* for another. What *lagom*
does, however, is transfer the focus from an individual
to a group context. Decisions are made based on what
is most appropriate for the situation and with a larger
perspective than just the individual. The first written
reference to the word *lagom* appeared in the 1600s but
it is believed to have existed for centuries before.

JANTELAGEN: THE JANTE LAW

Related to the idea of *lagom* is a concept called
Jantelagen. Every culture is underpinned by a set of
social principles governing the day-to-day behavior of
people. In his novel *A Fugitive Crosses His Tracks*, the
early twentieth-century Danish-Norwegian author Aksel
Sandemose listed ten oppressive laws designed to keep
people in their places in the imaginary Nordic village
of "Jante."

The first of these was "Thou shalt not believe thou
art something." The remaining laws admonished the
reader not to think of himself as wiser, better, more
knowledgeable, or more important than anyone else.
Additionally, he should not *ever* believe that he would
amount to anything or think that anyone cared about

him. Although intended as a satire, this bleak depiction of Scandinavian social norms was so accurate that the novel had a profound effect on its readers, and the contemporary Swedish traits of modesty, humility, and self-restraint are direct reflections of the Jante Law.

In today's Sweden, the Jante Law creates a generational and geographical divide. Some older Swedes, especially those in rural areas, may still reflect the Jante Law oppression of their younger days. They may go to great lengths to appear to be no better than anyone else because this would not be fair or equitable. It might extend to the way they dress (no flashiness), their cars, homes, and their demeanor in public (no boisterous behavior). The potential consequence of standing out could be the public humiliation of being cut down to size.

Younger Swedes and many in urban areas, however, dismiss the Jante Law mentality as a remnant of the past. In the large cities such as Stockholm you will see expensive cars, designer clothes, and other overt displays of wealth and status. It is no longer vulgar to be a high achiever or a high earner in Sweden. Boasting about it, on the other hand, is generally seen as tacky and unsophisticated. And Jante rears its head anyway and demands that a balance be struck. Talking about your status is acceptable, as long as you do it *lagom*.

UnSwedishness
In most places around the world, being regarded as a typical representative of your country is seen as

something good. In Sweden, however, the opposite often applies. Because of the legacy of *Jante* and *lagom* many Swedes reject their reserved stereotype and admire expressive, colorful, lively, spontaneous people, who are seen as exotic and the opposite of what Sweden is. There is nothing more positive for a Swede than to be described as "unSwedish."

HARMONY OVER CONFRONTATION

Most Swedes prefer harmony to confrontation. This means many business meetings or even conversations at home strive to achieve a decision palatable to all through discussion and compromise, rather than voting along black and white lines. This process can be time consuming and frustrating for non-Swedes wanting quick decisions.

Swedes tend to view confrontation as a situation that should be managed. As self-expression is also a strong value in Sweden, this can be a tricky balance, which is where harmony comes into play. Saying what you think is clearly not the same as agreeing, so listening to each other requires no confrontation in theory. The view is that mature adults should be able to navigate their differences. To others this might look like conflict avoidance, but to a Swede it is seen as showing respect for each other and striving for harmony.

Generally, Swedes put great value on a verbal agreement, and once having given approval consider themselves honor-bound to uphold it. The judicial system supports this in that witnessed verbal agreements are legally binding.

THE HONEST SWEDE

Maintaining harmony does not come at the expense of honesty, which is also a strong value in Swedish society. People who overembellish and exaggerate may be met with suspicion. Saying what you think can come across as brutal to people from other cultures, but for Swedes frankness is a way to build trust and gain respect. If what is said expresses a personal perception, it is valid, and does therefore not need to lead to a conflict. The bar for what you can say is very high. However, if Swedes perceive a confrontation they become less direct in their language and style.

Honesty also manifests itself in social behavior. Of course, lying and thieving exist in Sweden, but in general people try to be as honest as possible. If you drop a glove in the street in winter, just retrace your steps—you will find it placed on a bench ready for you to retrieve. Likewise, if you lose your wallet or cell phone in a café or store, there is a good chance that it will have been handed in at the cashier's desk by an honest Swede. If you go bathing in the summer, you can usually leave your bag and all its contents on the beach and assume that when you return everything will still be there. People who come from less trusting cultures may consider this naïve, but for Swedes personal honesty is essential for a respectful and secure society.

ORDERLINESS AND SECURITY

Sweden is a relatively safe country, and this is largely due to the prioritization of orderliness and security. Streets are generally well-lit and safe, public transportation usually runs on time, and people, in most situations, will stand in line to wait their turn. The Swedes developed the system of taking a numbered ticket, called a *nummerlapp*, dispensed from a machine, to keep people waiting in an orderly line.

Other famous Swedish inventions such as the safety belt, the safety match, the walking frame, the pacemaker, and the zipper, all reflect the value placed on personal security. And of course, the social safety net of the "Swedish Model" provides government-guaranteed security in the form of state pensions, healthcare, day care, workers' rights, and education.

According to a recent report, however, approximately one-third of Swedes feel unsafe in their local area. From relatively low levels, social unrest and crime—burglary, riots in city suburbs, gang shootings, and armed robbery—are on the rise. This has led to demands for stricter laws, improved policing, and harsher sentences. The question of crime and punishment has become a major battleground between the political parties.

THE SWEDISH MODEL

The Swedish welfare state was introduced in 1932 and further developed during the following five decades thanks to the country's strong economy. After the Second World War, Sweden quickly turned from arms manufacturing to producing the goods desperately needed by its war-torn neighbors. Additionally, Sweden is a highly industrialized country, rich in raw materials, including water sources for hydroelectric power, huge forests, and rich deposits of iron ore in the north.

The Swedish Model was the structure that provided citizens with economic protection throughout their lives. While it has undoubtedly created a socially secure society, this "cradle to grave" safety net has been criticized by some as creating a "nanny state" of complacent people. A project of such magnitude needs financing, and this is achieved through taxation. Sweden's taxes are among the highest in the world, ranging from 0 to 57 percent, depending on what you earn. The average income tax level is approximately 32 percent. Although people complain about high taxation, most are mindful of what they receive in return—parental leave, employment rights, unemployment benefit, sickness benefit, pensions, free education, and subsidized healthcare, to mention a few.

ATTITUDES TOWARD THE MONARCHY

According to a survey in 2016, approximately 25 percent of the population wanted to abolish the monarchy, the main argument being that it was an anachronism that had no place in a modern, equality-driven society. The rest of the population supported, or at least, tolerated the institution. The monarch has no constitutional power, and the role of King Carl XVI Gustaf and German-born Queen Silvia is mostly ceremonial, to preside at official state functions and to represent the country in a public relations capacity. Their official residence is the Royal Palace in Stockholm's Old Town and their permanent home is Drottningholm Palace outside Stockholm, both of which are well worth a visit. They have three children, Princess Victoria, Prince Carl Philip, and Princess Madeleine. There are also many royal grandchildren.

As Sweden has a gender-neutral succession, the heir apparent is Crown Princess Victoria, who will eventually become the first female monarch since Queen Ulrika Eleonora (1718–20). In 2010, Princess Victoria married her personal trainer, now called Prince Daniel, in a very popular and internationally televised wedding ceremony. She has three children, of whom Princess Estelle is next in line to the throne. Together Victoria and Estelle will secure decades of female regnancy in Sweden.

In 2019, in a move to modernize the monarchy and reduce costs, King Carl Gustaf relieved five of his grandchildren of their royal duties. They have kept

King Carl Gustaf and Queen Silvia on a visit to Skansen in 2016.

their titles but lost the HRH prefix and are no longer members of the royal house. This also means they no longer receive any financial support from the state.

The Swedish nobility still exists, totaling about 26,000 members, although today they have no special privileges. The King's right to grant noble status ended with the constitutional reform of 1974. Names, titles, and coats of arms are protected. Family coats of arms are on display at the Church of the Nobility (Riddarkyrkan) and in the Swedish House of Nobility (Riddarhuset) in Stockholm's Old Town.

It's All in the Name

Although nobility confers no official privileges, having a noble name can bring social status and special treatment among certain groups. Interesting noble family names include:

Björn (Bear)
Bonde (Farmer)
Leijonhufvud (Lion Head)
Natt och Dag (Night and Day)
Svinhufvud (Pig Head)
Trolle (Troll)
Örnsparre (Eagle Arrow)

ATTITUDE TOWARD NATURE

Ask a Swede who owns nature and the answer will be "all of us." This attitude is rooted strongly in the concept of "*Allemansrätt*," or the Right to Roam. The right of public access to certain public or privately owned land, lakes, and rivers for recreation and exercise, if it does not disturb the owner or result in any destruction of property, is guaranteed in the constitution. Sailors may anchor and use beaches, hikers may hike, campers may camp for one night, and anyone can walk through the forests and pick mushrooms and berries. In recent years, *Allemansrätten* has come under attack as foreign pickers empty the forests of berries and mushrooms to sell at markets. Like much else in Sweden, the picking of nature's treasures should also be *lagom*—just take what you need and nothing more.

The Swedish Environmental Protection Agency has produced a six-page brochure outlining the dos and dont's (see www.swedishepa.se/). Here are a few:

- You can pitch your tent for a night or two in the countryside as long as you don't disturb the landowner or damage the surroundings.
- You can walk or ski almost everywhere in nature. However, you must be careful not to disturb anyone or destroy anything.
- It is important that you choose a spot for your campfire where there's no risk of it spreading or causing damage to soil and vegetation. Gravel or sandy ground is best.

Camping in the wild.

Most Swedes enjoy walking in the open air whenever they get the opportunity, and who can blame them? The country is blessed with magnificent forests, untouched lakes, and impressive mountains. The air is fresh, the water clean. In the great outdoors people find a space for reverence and contemplation. Some say that the forest has replaced the Church for many Swedes—creating a new kind of contemporary religion. This theory is explored further in David Thurfjell's 2020 book *Pine Forest People*.

SEXUAL FREEDOM

Without the religious dogma that exists in other countries, the Swedes have a pragmatic attitude toward relationships, sex, and marriage. The age of consent is fifteen and most parents are comfortable having open discussions with their children about sexual health. Many are relaxed about their teenagers' partners sleeping over. Sexual Education is compulsory in all schools.

Dating online and via apps is very common—Tinder, Grinder, and Happy Pancake being the most popular. When dating, it is common to meet for a drink or a coffee rather than dinner so that it is easier to leave if the date is not going as expected. Casual sexual encounters among Swedes, by both men and women, are perfectly acceptable.

You must be eighteen to get married in Sweden without parental consent. Forced marriage is illegal, and since 1995 marriage in Sweden has been gender neutral. Marriage has recently become more popular, with approximately 50,000 couples tying the knot every year.

It is common for people to cohabit in Sweden—a romantic and practical way of coping with high living costs in the expensive cities. It is also very common to have children without being married. The Cohabitants Act protects partners in the case of death.

When it comes to divorce, the Swedish system is equally pragmatic. In Sweden, you can divorce the person you are married to even if s/he does not want to. You just make a divorce application. If there are children under the age of sixteen involved, you will be given six months to a year to consider your decision.

ATTITUDES TOWARD HOMOSEXUALITY

As we have seen, the rights of LGBTQA people are enshrined in law, and the Swedes are generally very open and accepting of individuals with a non-normative sexual orientation. However, people in rural areas or with traditional conservative values may have a more negative attitude. Hate crimes do occur and violence against the transgender community is unfortunately increasing. Younger Swedes tend to be more open toward gender and sexual fluidity than previous generations.

Women police officers in the Stockholm Pride parade, 2019.

WORK–LIFE BALANCE

Historically, Swedes were taught via Lutheranism that hard work builds character and brings redemption. Today's Swede has a different focus—one of trying to find the best work–life balance possible. Companies invest heavily in employee satisfaction to help individuals stay balanced, by, for example, installing table tennis tables, providing chillout rooms, and organizing frequent "fun" conferences in Sweden and abroad. The standard working week is 40 hours, with office hours generally starting around 8:00 a.m. and ending around 6:00 p.m. Many companies have flexitime, which provides employees with a lot of freedom to come and go. Parents of small children often leave at around 4:00 p.m. Swedes have thirteen national holidays. The minimum number of vacation days is twenty-five, with a minimum of three weeks allowed to be taken in a row. Most Swedes take their vacations in June–August, when the weather is best, and then again in the winter when they flee the country.

Freedom With Responsibility

The Swedish concept of *"frihet under ansvar"* (freedom with responsibility) is practiced in most companies. Provided you achieve your goals, how you achieve them is less important—in other words, there is great freedom to plan your own time and work schedule. This usually removes the need for micromanagement and results in a workforce that has a lot more flexibility than many other places around the world. However, this is not to say that Swedes do not get stressed. There is, in fact, a high incidence of burnout and stress-related illness in the Swedish workplace.

During the coronavirus pandemic of 2020, people were instructed to work from home if they could. The concept of *frihet under ansvar* made this possible. Approximately one-third of the working population switched to home working, and statistics showed that productivity increased.

One would think that the prioritization of work–life balance would affect motivation negatively. While there are certainly individuals who freeload and abuse the system, most Swedes are dedicated to, and very motivated by, their work.

Despite the benefits of a good work–life balance, Sweden faces challenges going into the future. High taxes and labor regulations can make the country less competitive internationally. High rents and a lack of housing in the bigger cities make it hard to attract young talent. Sweden's dark and cold winters can also make it hard to attract labor. On the other hand, the harsh winters are often referred to as an explanation for the high level of creativity in Sweden—the long, cold season encourages would-be innovators to stay indoors to hone their skills and develop their ideas.

Regarding innovation and entrepreneurship, the fact that the welfare state provides a social safety net to fall back on if a venture fails offers entrepreneurs the freedom to experiment and take risks. In 2020, Sweden topped the European Innovation Scoreboard and was in the top echelon of the Global Innovation Index.

SOME INTERNATIONALLY SUCCESSFUL SWEDISH COMPANIES:

• Spotify • Ericsson • H&M • Ikea • Oatly • Volvo
• Electrolux • Absolut • Rekorderlig
• J Lindeberg • Hasselblad

Praise and Humility

Once at a work meeting, I thanked a colleague for doing a great job. I expected her to accept the compliment graciously. Instead, she responded that she was just doing what she was responsible for and did not appreciate being singled out in that way. That's when I learned that for many Swedes it is not appropriate to offer compliments or praise in front of the team. In recent years this has changed, but many Swedes still find it awkward to be set apart from the group. It could be the ghost of Jante still hanging around.

ATTITUDES TOWARD OTHERS

Levels of trust are very high Swede-to-Swede. This intuitive trust extends, to some degree, to other Europeans and Americans, but tends to decrease in relation to people from other countries. That said, Sweden still remains a high-trust culture in comparison to many other societies. Whether this will be affected by the immigration of people from less trusting cultures remains to be seen. In general, the Swedes are very open and welcoming to tourists and visitors and will be friendly and helpful if approached.

CHAPTER THREE

CUSTOMS & TRADITIONS

The Swedes celebrate their customs and traditions with gusto. These often involve the eating of similar festive foods, the imbibing of *snaps*, and the singing of traditional drinking songs. Many customs have a pagan origin; others are rooted in Christianity. A few, including May 1 and National Day, are secular. While the Swedes cherish their native historical festivals, they are also open to integrating non-Swedish traditions. Imported holidays such as Valentine's Day, St. Patrick's Day, and Halloween have grown in popularity in recent years.

THE SWEDISH YEAR

Thirteen of the many official days of celebration are national holidays, called "red days" in Swedish as they are printed red in calendars. In the table overleaf the "red day" holidays appear in bold type.

DATE	SWEDISH HOLIDAY	ENGLISH NAME
January 1	**Nyårsdagen**	New Year's Day
January 6	**Trettondedag Jul**	Epiphany
January 13	Tjugondedag Knut	Knut Hilarymas
February/March	Fastlag (Fettisdag)	Lent (ShroveTuesday)
March/April	Skärtorsdag	Maundy Thursday ("Clean" Thursday)
March/April	**Långfredagen**	Good Friday ("Long" Friday)
March/April	**Påskdagen**	Easter Day
March/April	**Annandag Påsk**	Easter Monday ("Another" Easter Day)
April 30	Valborgsmässoafton	Walpurgis Night
May 1	**Första Maj**	May Day
Middle/end of May	**Kristi Himmelsfärdsdag**	Ascension Day
Last Sunday in May	Mors dag	Mother's Day
May/June	**Pingstdagen**	Whitsun
June 6	**Sveriges nationaldag**	Sweden's National Day
End of June	**Midsommarsdagen**	Midsummer Day
A Saturday between 31 Oct. – 6 Nov.	**Alla Helgons dag**	All Saints' Day
November 11	Mårtensgås	St. Martin's Day
Second Sunday in Nov.	Fars dag	Father's Day
4th Sunday before Christmas	Advent	Advent
December 10	Nobeldagen	Nobel Day
December 13	Luciadagen	Lucia
December 24	Julafton	Christmas Eve
December 25	**Juldagen**	Christmas
December 26	**Annandag Jul**	Boxing Day
December 31	Nyårsafton	New Year's Eve

FESTIVALS, TRADITIONS, AND HOLIDAYS

Name Days

In Sweden, each day of the year has a first name associated with it. For example, January 2 is Svea and December 31 is Sylvester. In the past people would receive a present on their name day but today it is celebrated with a text, a post on somebody's social media, or maybe a phone call.

January
New Year's Day

New Year's Day is a quiet event in Sweden and the day that most takeout pizzas are sold. However, as in many places around the world, the evening before, New Year's Eve, is a big celebration. Friends and families gather to eat and make merry and watch the fireworks at midnight. After midnight, a small meal is eaten, which can vary from hotdogs to lobster. Every year, in a ritual dating back to 1895, a famous actor reads aloud a translation of the poem "Ring Out, Wild Bells" by Alfred, Lord Tennyson, on the stage at Skansen, Stockholm's open-air museum. As the poem is recited and televised to the nation, the bells ring out over the city and fireworks echo in the night sky.

Epiphany (Trettondedag Jul)

The holy day of Epiphany (Trettondedag Jul), literally "thirteenth day Christmas," on January 6, is a legal holiday, and in many countries marks the end of the

Semlor buns on Shrove Tuesday.

long Christmas holiday period. Traditionally, however, Swedes, prolonged the festivities by a week, until January 13, when people would come together to strip the tree of its ornaments, play games, eat, drink, and generally have fun. This occasion is known as Tjugondedag Knut, the twentieth day after Christmas. Today, the Swedes take down the decorations and throw out the tree whenever is most convenient—usually at a weekend.

February
Fettisdagen, or Shrove Tuesday, is celebrated with the eating of Lent buns filled with almond paste and topped with whipped cream. Known as a *semla* (plural *semlor*), these delicious buns are among the most popular pastries in Sweden. So popular is the *semla* that it appears in bakeries just after the New

Year and disappears some time at the end of March.
Traditionalists are often appalled by this and insist the
buns be eaten on Shrove Tuesday only!

March–April
Easter (Påsk)

The pagan and the sacred are intermingled at Easter. On
Maundy Thursday, children tie headscarves over their
heads, paint their faces, wear long skirts, and go door-
to-door dressed as colorful witches begging for sweets.
Swedish folklore has it that at Easter the witches fly to
visit the devil on Blue Mountain (Blåkulla) and must
be kept from returning. The treats are said to appease
them. In some communities, bonfires are symbolically
lit on the Saturday before Easter to keep the witches at
bay. Everyone loves painting Easter eggs.

Not so frightening Easter "witches."

The days, while still cold, are increasingly sunny.
Birch twigs are brought indoors and decorated with
brightly dyed feathers and colorful egg ornaments. One
theory, among many, is that twigs represent the witches'
broomsticks and the feathers the idea of flight.

With few people attending church regularly, the four days
off at Easter represent a welcome opportunity to squeeze in
one last ski trip, open up the country house, do some spring
cleaning, or start preparing the boat for the water.

The traditional Easter foods include salmon, boiled
eggs filled with caviar or shrimps, and pickled herring.
Some people eat lamb, others go for a ham.

Walpurgis Night (Valborgsmässoafton)
April 30, also the birthday of King Carl XVI Gustaf, is
the eve of the feast of St. Walburga, when people gather

Walpurgis night bonfire in Stockholm, with the City Hall in the background.

in front of bonfires all over Sweden to sing songs welcoming spring. More often than not, it is raining, sleeting, or otherwise miserable weather. Walpurgis is a big drinking and reveling night among the young, as the following day is a public holiday.

May
May Day
May 1, Labor Day in much of Europe, originates in the workers' rights movement and is a legal holiday. It is usually a calm, ceremonial occasion. Representatives and members of most of the political parties and labor unions gather under their respective banners to march through the streets and listen to speeches in a nearby park. Swedes who are not interested in these events usually treat the occasion as a welcome day off and a chance to meet up at an outdoor café.

Ascension Day (Kristi Himmelsfärdsdag)
This falls five and a half weeks after Easter, usually in May. Because it is always on a Thursday many Swedes take the Friday off (known as a "*klämdag*" or a "squeeze day").

June
National Day
Sweden's National Day on June 6 marks the accession to the throne of Gustav I Vasa in 1523. A ceremony is held at Skansen open-air museum-park in Stockholm, where the monarch presents flags to representatives

At the National Day celebrations in Norrköping, eastern Sweden, 2014.

of various civic groups. The monarch also invites the public to visit large parts of Stockholm Palace, which is open all day without the usual entry fees. Up and down the country, Swedish flags are flown and local authorities arrange public events.

Midsummer

Midsummer's Eve is probably the most important celebration in the Swedish calendar. Celebrated on the Friday of the weekend closest to June 24, it is a time of twenty-four-hour sunlight in the far north. Towns empty as people head out to their country houses, and many shops and restaurants are closed for business.

Early in the day, wildflowers are gathered to be hung from the maypole or woven into wreaths to be worn on the head. All gather around to sing traditional songs and dance, sometimes to the accompaniment of an accordion and a fiddle. A *smörgåsbord* of pickled herring, crispbread, and new potatoes follows, interspersed with singing, drinking, and toasting with

Dancing around the maypole on Midsummer in the market town of Olofström.

snaps—a potent, flavored, relative of vodka. This means that Midsummer is often a raucous and sometimes uninhibited celebration, which includes skinny-dipping in the cold waters. Dessert is fresh strawberries and cream or ice cream. According to folklore, a maiden who places seven different wildflowers under her pillow before falling asleep will dream of her future husband.

August
The Crayfish Party
Mid-August through early September is the time for crayfish parties, if possible outdoors. The crayfish are cooked in salted water and fresh dill and eating them entails much slurping and sucking to remove the crayfish meat from the bright red shells. This, in turn, necessitates a round of *snaps*, drinking songs, and beer chasers, so the crayfish party is often a drunken affair. People wear conical (and comical) party hats and paper bibs, and string paper lanterns shaped like smiling full moons from the trees or parasols.

The Fermented Herring (Surströmming) Premiere

You may have seen "challenge" videos on YouTube in which the contestants attempt to eat smelly fish while gagging, swearing, and throwing up. What they are eating is the Swedish specialty *surströmming*, or fermented herring, which is very much an acquired taste and which most Swedes give a miss. Those who do enjoy it eat the rotten fish outdoors with *snaps*, flat bread, boiled potato, sour cream, and cheese. The fish comes in a bulging tin that looks set to explode due to the fermentation process. Opening the container, therefore, is an art in itself. The stench that arises is both pungent and stomach-churning and therefore the tin should never be opened indoors. *Surströmming* originated in the 1500s as a cheap food eaten by poor people. In the 1800s it was taken up by the richer classes and earned its reputation as a delicacy.

October
All Saints' Day (Alla Helgons Dag)

All Saints' Day is celebrated on the first Saturday after October 30. People place wreaths and special, long-burning candles on the graves of departed loved ones or in the memory grove.

November
St. Martin's Day

This feast day, on November 11, is most popular in the southern county of Skåne. It originally celebrated the memory of St. Martin of Tours, but eventually came to honor Martin Luther. It is not a legal holiday. Roast goose is typically served, preceded by a bowl of dark soup made from goose-blood and spices.

December
Advent
On the four Sundays preceding Christmas, the Swedes light Advent candles, one extra candle being lit each week. They also place electric advent candle holders in their windows to light up the darkness, and these can stay in place well into February. There are many colorful Christmas markets in the town squares during Advent. There are also festive open-house parties where hot mulled wine (*glögg*) and gingersnap cookies (*pepparkakor*) are served.

Lucia (St. Lucy's Day)
If you are fortunate enough to be in Sweden on December 13, and are up early enough, you will witness a beautiful Swedish tradition. In the early hours of the morning Santa Lucia walks the streets, dressed in a white robe with a red sash around her waist and a metal circlet of lighted candles on her head. Together with her white-clad handmaidens and other followers, she slowly brings light to the darkness. This illuminated procession pauses to hold concerts in churches up and down the country, and visits workplaces, hospitals, and old peoples' homes. *Glögg* is often drunk and saffron buns known as *lussekatter* are eaten.

The origin of the Lucia tradition is hard to determine. It seems to be a blending of the story of the Christian

martyr Lucia of Syracuse and the Swedish legend of
Lucia as Adam's first wife. Today, it is a festival that
almost all children and young adults participate in, and
most Swedes know the lyrics to all the Lucia hymns and
songs. Lucia herself is traditionally female, and elected
by classmates. The festival tends, however, to bring out
the worst in traditionalists. On the rare occasions that
a boy has been elected to play the coveted role there
have been vociferous protests. Interestingly, the very
first Lucia, in the 1820s, was in fact a man. When a
dark-skinned boy portrayed Lucia in advertising for the
Swedish department store Åhléns in 2016, around three
hundred hateful and racist comments were posted on
Facebook. It seems that having a non-white, male Lucia
was just too much for some people.

Christmas (Jul)

Christmas is celebrated on Christmas Eve and people
exchange presents, called *julklapp*. Many Swedish homes
have a straw goat (*julbock*), in a nod to the Middle Ages
when presents were distributed by a goat. Christmas
Eve usually begins with a breakfast consisting of rice
porridge, *vörtbröd* (spiced malt bread), and cheese.
Then a long wait begins until 3:00 p.m., when most
families gather in front of the TV to watch the Walt
Disney Christmas special "From All of Us to All of You."
In Sweden, the program is known colloquially as *Kalle
Anka*, Donald Duck, and it has been broadcast every year
since 1959. When the program ends, Father Christmas
(*Tomten*) arrives to distribute presents. Tomten is usually

a parent, friend, or neighbor disguised in a red robe, fake beard, and hat. In some families, each present is accompanied by a rhyme or riddle, which must be solved before the gift can be opened.

The traditional Christmas late lunch/early dinner follows: a buffet table (*smörgåsbord*) groaning with pickled herring (*sill*), smoked salmon, liver pâté, smoked sausages, and cold spare ribs; crisp, unleavened bread and an array of cheeses; plus the hot dishes of miniature hotdogs, meatballs, Jansson's Temptation (a gratin casserole of potatoes and anchovies), red cabbage spiced with cloves, and the Christmas ham. Dessert may simply be a bowl of fresh fruit or a creamed rice dessert called "Ris a la Malta." Adults usually drink beer or wine with *snaps*. The shotting of *snaps* is accompanied by traditional drinking songs with everybody joining in.

That evening, if you're still hungry, a dish of *Lutfisk* can be eaten. This is a type of cod that has been dried, rehydrated in a lye solution, then further soaked in cold water and boiled to a jellylike consistency. It is served smothered in melted butter and/or a cream sauce.

Christmas Day itself begins for some with a very early morning church service. It is often a family day, spent with jigsaw puzzles, board games, books, long walks, or visits to the cinema. What is eaten on Christmas Day is less traditional, with some people eating the leftovers from the day before and others preferring goose, turkey, or even a takeout.

Annandag Jul (Boxing Day)

December 26 is also a legal holiday and for most people is spent relaxing. It is also a popular day to fly away to warmer climes to celebrate New Year in the sun.

INTERNATIONAL AWARD CEREMONIES

Sweden has its fair share of national prize ceremonies for film, theater, music, and more. There are also three internationally renowned awards that originate in Sweden.

Polar Music Prize: May

The late Stig Anderson, Abba's manager and lyricist, created the Polar Music Prize to honor exceptional achievements in the creation and advancement of music. The prize, one million Swedish Crowns, is awarded by the King of Sweden each May in a televised ceremony. Winners of the Polar Prize have included the likes of Metallica, Paul McCartney, and Joni Mitchell.

Stockholm Water Prize: August

Another award presented by the King is the Stockholm Water Prize. This is awarded to a person or organization that contributes to the conservation and protection of water resources, and to the well-being of the planet and its inhabitants. A prize ceremony and royal banquet is held at the Stockholm City Hall as part of World Water Week in August.

Nobel Day: December 10

Established in 1896, the Nobel Prize acknowledges excellence in literature, physics, chemistry, medicine, and physiology at a special ceremony in Stockholm each year on December 10. The Nobel Prize is considered the most prestigious award in the world. Prizewinners have included Albert Einstein, Marie Curie, and Toni Morrison. The Nobel Prize is the legacy of Alfred Nobel, the Swedish industrialist, engineer, chemist, and inventor of dynamite, who was born on October 21, 1833, and died on December 10, 1896.

Upon his death, Nobel bequeathed his assets of 31 million Swedish crowns to a fund to be distributed annually as prizes to "those who, during the preceding year, shall have conferred the greatest benefit on mankind."

To celebrate the esteemed laureates, a grand banquet is held in Stockholm City Hall. The speeches, performances, and the eating of the banquet is broadcast live. Some Swedes even gather in front of their televisions, dress up, and eat their own sumptuous dinners simultaneously. (The Nobel Peace Prize is awarded in a similar ceremony in Oslo.)

FAMILY OCCASIONS

Birth, Baptism, and Confirmation

Around 40 percent of Swedish children are baptized and under 30 percent of all fifteen-year-olds elect to be confirmed. Following the christening and confirmation ceremonies, friends and relatives attend a reception at home or in the church hall, bringing presents.

Graduation

Graduation from *gymnasium*, the Swedish equivalent of the American high school, is a rite of passage. On graduation day family and friends gather outside the school in groups with a large placard or poster on a tall stick, bearing an enlarged photo of the graduate at a young age. When, after the valedictory ceremony, the graduates run out of the school building, they are cheered by the crowd outside. After this, they climb onto the backs of open lorries and trucks and drive through the streets with music booming and drink flowing. They eventually arrive at the family reception their parents are giving in their honor, and later move on for a party of their own.

Engagement

Engaged couples exchange engagement rings, worn on the left hand. A second ring is exchanged at the wedding.

Sometime before the wedding day, friends of the betrothed couple "kidnap" him or her for a day, all in great fun, and put them through various amusing situations in public, with varying degrees of humiliation. This usually ends with dinner and drinks.

Weddings

In Sweden, marriage is equal for all, irrespective of sexual orientation. Church weddings make up one-third of all weddings in the country, the rest being civil ceremonies.

Priests have the right to decline to marry a same-sex couple. If that happens, the Church is obliged to help them find another priest. At a heterosexual church wedding, the couple usually walk up the aisle together, rather than the bride's father escorting her to the waiting groom at the altar, because a bride is not a possession to be handed over by one man to another.

The ceremony is followed by a reception, usually in another location, and the newlyweds, who are the last to arrive, stay quite late to enjoy the fun. During the proceedings anyone can make a speech or sing a song and there is usually a Toastmaster or Toastmadame to coordinate this. This can mean that the reception takes a long time to conclude. Women guests do not wear black at weddings, which would be considered bad luck.

Birthdays
Being pragmatic people, the Swedes often assume responsibility for their own birthday celebrations. At work, a person usually brings in their own cake and invites colleagues to join in.

Birthdays ending in a "0" are milestones and particularly important. It is popular to celebrate these with parties, speeches, performances, and toasting. Presents are usually not over-the-top lavish—perhaps a gift voucher, an experience, or a bottle of bubbly.

Funerals
Death notices are published in the newspaper, giving the time and location of the church service. Many people

today are cremated—a practical solution, since months can go by before the ground has thawed enough for the deceased to be buried.

Mourners file past the coffin, which may be open or closed. As they pass, they lay a single flower on top of it, look solemnly and reflectively down, and then continue around and back to the pew.

RELIGION

The Church of Sweden has been separated from the state since 2000, which means that there is no longer an official state Church, unlike the neighboring Nordic countries. Although Sweden has moved from being a Lutheran to a secular country, 58 percent of the population remain (mostly passive) members of the

Constructed like a stylized Sámi tent, the wooden church in Kiruna with its free-standing bell tower is regarded as "the Shrine of the Nomadic People."

Swedish Church. As such, they pay 1 percent of their income in tax to preserve the 3,700 churches around the country and to maintain traditions such as baptisms, weddings, funerals, and festive concerts. After the Church of Sweden, the Free Churches (*frikyrkor*) are the next largest religious group. Free Churches are independent Protestant organizations based on Evangelical, Pentecostal, Methodist, and Baptist traditions. The area around the city of Jönköping is known as the "Swedish Bible Belt" because of its high level of Free Church activity. There are also vibrant and active communities of other religions, such as Judaism, Hinduism, Sikhism, and Buddhism.

Islam

The largest non-Christian religious group is Muslim, and Sweden has nine purpose-built mosques—the first was built in Malmö in 1984. There are no official statistics on religion in Sweden, as registering people's religious beliefs is illegal, but it is estimated that there are around 200,000 Muslims.

Most Muslims in Sweden originally came from Iraq, Iran, Bosnia-Herzegovina, Turkey, Lebanon, and Kosovo. Most of the Iranians and Iraqis arrived as refugees during the Iran–Iraq War, from 1980 to 1988. The second-largest group consists of immigrants or refugees from Eastern Europe, particularly from the former Yugoslavia. There is also a sizeable community of Somalis. They are followed by refugees from Syria and Afghanistan, two rapidly growing groups.

CHAPTER FOUR

MAKING FRIENDS

In Sweden friendship is valued very highly, and if you have a Swedish friend, you have them for life. Although some may be gregarious and have wide social networks, most Swedes are content with a small circle of close friends. It is not unusual for them to still socialize with people they went to kindergarten or school with. The tight-knit nature of Swedish friendship groups can make it difficult for outsiders to break into the inner circle, particularly as many Swedes consider that they do not have the time to invest in developing new friendships. When they do want to make new friends, they tend to do this at work, social events, or through organized sports or special-interest clubs (see overleaf).

Although you are unlikely to make instant friends when you visit Sweden as a tourist, you will find that most people are friendly and helpful. However, they will probably not stop and offer to help you if you appear to be lost; they will assume you are capable of solving the problem yourself or else asking for assistance. The level of English is generally extremely high, thanks to the Swedish school system and the fact that English-speaking TV programs are subtitled and not dubbed.

WORK AND SOCIAL LIFE

Work and private life are mostly kept separate, although going out on a Friday after work (the so-called "AW") is popular among singles, and people do find romantic partners among their colleagues. People with children or partners often rush home to start *fredagsmys*, which translates as "Friday cosiness." This usually involves family time in front of the television, eating crisps and fast food such as pizza or taco. Eating taco is so common that the concept of "Taco Friday" has emerged.

In Swedish firms team building is an important part of company life. Employers invest in corporate parties, outings, or weekend getaways (no spouses) as a way of bringing people together on a personal level. Professional networking events are also very popular, although some individuals might find this form of mingling awkward.

Meeting new people and socializing outside the inner circle usually takes place in sports clubs or special interest associations. Sweden has a very rich *föreningsliv* (club life) of organized group activities. These can include anything from playing a particular sport to learning a new language, participating in a

Groups of friends enjoying the good weather in Stockholm.

book club, or joining a choir. If you want to get to know Swedes, joining a club or association is strongly recommended.

Sports

In general, the Swedes are a sporty bunch, and joining in is a great way to meet them. In the winter, gyms and sport halls are packed, and team sports such as *innebandy* (floorball), basketball, handball, and five-a-side football are popular. Racquet sports such as squash and badminton are also common. A new racquet sport is the Mexican game padel, similar to the US "paddle tennis," with courts springing up all over the country. In the summer, you'll see people running and kayaking on the many trails and lakes up and

Innebandy, or floorball, is a fast-moving type of indoor floor hockey.

down the country. Golf has a wide following, and a significant half a million Swedes are members of a golf club.

Joining In
The Swedes are great joiners. To make friends, non-Swedes can also join one of the following groups, which are easy to find on the Internet:
- Nya Kompisbyrån, which aims to help new arrivals meet Swedes over a coffee or a dinner.
- Little Bear Abroad. Helps international families feel at home in Sweden by organizing events such as picnics and meet-ups.
- Internationella Bekantskaper is an association that matches people who speak Swedish with people who are learning Swedish.

- Kompis Sverige matches Swedes with non-Swedes, with the aim of creating lasting friendships.
- Internations is a networking organization for expats from different countries to meet each other.
- Various Chambers of Commerce.

> ### *Dating Etiquette*
> Net dating and app dating are widespread in Sweden. Commonly used apps are Tinder, Grindr, Badoo, and Happy Pancake. Interested parties usually meet for a hook-up, a walk, a coffee, or a drink rather than a dinner. If you do dine out, it is not unusual to split the bill afterward, or for each person just to pay for what they've eaten. This releases them from any sense of obligation or preconceived notion as to how the evening might end. Casual romantic encounters are common as the Swedes are generally not prudish about sex.

CLOTHING

The way Swedes dress covers the entire spectrum of fashion. You'll find people who prefer casual clothes and others who are very fashion-conscious and cutting-edge. One thing most Swedes have in common is that they are usually well groomed and well turned out. Visitors to the country are often struck by how nice looking and well dressed the Swedes are. In Sweden it is very acceptable, particularly among young urban men, to take an interest in your personal appearance. Many Swedish men are comfortable purchasing unisex products for hair care, bath, and shower, and there are make-up products specifically tailored for men, such as concealer. Sweden has produced many international fashion labels such as H&M, Cheap Monday, Filippa K, Tiger, Acne, and Nudie.

In the workplace, dress is usually casual, depending on where you work. It is acceptable to wear jeans and T-shirts to the office. You may even see people wearing clogs or Birkenstocks for comfort. Suits and formal wear are normally reserved for more traditional occupations, such as law or banking.

In Swedish there is an expression, "There is no bad weather—only bad clothes." Warm clothing, hats, gloves, and insulated boots are essential in the winter. A second pair of shoes is often brought and put on indoors so that you do not bring in the dirt and slush.

Dressing Up

While work wear might be more casual, going out usually requires a little more dressing up. If invited to a party, Swedish men may don a jacket and maybe a tie, or opt for a fashionable shirt and dark jeans. Women will wear trendy outfits with glitter and strong prints, or a classic black dress. For both men and women, clothes tend to be darker in the winter months and brighter and more cheerful in the sunnier half of the year.

"Smart casual" is the norm for businessmen.

Invitations to formal dinner parties usually specify *kavaj* (which means dark suit or jacket for men). For women, it means a stylish dress or blouse and skirt.

Very dressy events, which are rare, are specified as *smoking*—tuxedo/black tie for a man and an evening gown for a woman.

GREETINGS

In Swedish, the word *Hej* (pronounced "hay") is hello and *Hej då* (pronounced "hay door") is goodbye. "*Hej*" can also be used to say goodbye, which can be confusing for the uninitiated. To say "please" or "thank you" just say "*Tack.*"

Swedes rarely address a person as Mr. or Mrs. First names are used. They are also not big on titles, such as "President" or "Managing Director."

In both business and social settings, it is customary to shake hands and simultaneously say your own name. In social settings, the most recent person arriving makes the rounds of those already present and introduces himself. This you do for groups of up to about ten people. Eye contact is important. Swedes who know each other will usually hug. Kissing is not a common way of greeting.

TOURIST-FRIENDLY SWEDES

In general, Swedes like visitors and are proud to show off their beautiful towns and countryside. Everybody speaks English, and many speak other languages such as German, Spanish, Persian, or Arabic. Naturally, learning the language of the host country is an advantage, and speaking Swedish is one of the best ways to achieve a better understanding of Swedish culture and a more successful integration. There are free Swedish courses for foreigners called SFI (Swedish for Immigrants).

INVITATIONS HOME

If you are invited home by a Swede, it is customary to bring a small gift, usually flowers, chocolate, or wine. When giving flowers, Swedes generally remove the florist's paper wrapping before knocking on your door.

If you are going to be more than fifteen minutes late, text or call your hosts and let them know. It is generally not acceptable to arrive early. You will be offered a "welcome drink" upon arrival before dinner.

If you are in a couple, and the seating is pre-determined, you will probably find that you are not placed next to your partner. This is to encourage the flow of conversation. You may also find that the host seats the guests in male/female order, if possible.

You may be offered a tour of your host's home, the so-called *husesyn*.

Take Your Shoes off at the Door

In most Swedish homes, it is customary to remove your shoes at the door to avoid tracking in water, mud, or gravel. So, if you are invited to a Swedish home, make sure your socks are clean and intact. Some people bring a pair of light shoes to change into. For Swedes this is a normal ritual, and many are appalled by Brits and Americans who wear their outdoor shoes indoors.

Etiquette

Eating is usually an informal affair in Sweden. Formal dinner etiquette, however, is quite ritualized. The guest of honor is seated on the left of the hostess, or, if there is no hostess, then the host. The man to the left of any female guest is her *kavaljer*, from the French *cavalier*, whose duty it is to attend to her needs. This escort service continues throughout the entire evening, not just at the dinner table.

Another social ritual is toasting. No one drinks before the host or hostess has proposed a toast, which they do by raising their glass of wine and offering a few welcoming words.

How to Toast in Sweden

Hold your glass near your breastbone at about the level of the third button on a shirt. Once your host or hostess has finished the welcome and said "*Skål!*" (pronounced "skoal"), raise your glass and tip it slightly toward him or her while saying the same thing. Slowly make eye contact with every single person around the table, one after the other. Then, in synchronization with your host or hostess, take one sip of the wine, return the glass to the chest-high position, and again make eye contact with him or her, and then with each guest around the table before putting your glass down. You are now free to drink at will and do not need to wait for further toasts. In situations where a song is involved, hold your glass at chest height during the entire song before taking your first sip.

Swedes eat with the fork in the left hand and the knife in the right. You may have your own butter knife, or it may be shared with the other guests. You will usually have several glasses in front of you—for wine, beer, water, and *snaps*.

While wine will be offered throughout the dinner, not everyone will drink. One reason for this is Sweden's strict drunk-driving laws. The blood alcohol limit is 0.2 mg/ml. For anyone caught with a higher level than this in the bloodstream the punishment is severe (see pages 149–50). Thus either one member of a couple is the designated driver or they take a taxi, in which case both can drink.

It is considered good manners to send a thank you to your hosts the following day. A simple phone call or a text with a smiling emoji will do.

FIKA—THE ART OF THE COFFEE BREAK

The Swedes are among the largest consumers of coffee in the world, drinking on average 3.2 cups of coffee per day. This means that one of the first words foreigners learn when moving to Sweden is "*fika*." It means coffee break with cake, but is more than just grabbing a cup of coffee—it is an important cultural phenomenon. *Fika* is a popular way to socialize, partly because it is much more relaxed than a sit-down dinner. Swedes often meet friends in local cafés and bakeries for a *fika*, or invite each other home to drink coffee and eat home-baked goods. Towns around Sweden have lots of artisan coffee shops and national chains offering the latest trends in coffee. The market is so hard to break into that coffee giant Starbucks didn't open its first shop until 2010, and continues to struggle to gain market share. In workplaces, morning and afternoon *fika* are usually organized so that everybody attends. It is a casual way to meet colleagues and tune in to the office gossip, and everybody is expected to join in.

CHAPTER FIVE

THE SWEDES AT HOME

QUALITY OF LIFE

The Swedes set great store by a modern, clean, and bright environment. Quality of life and standard of living are priorities. Swedish homes usually have modern interiors and are bright and clean. In the spring, windows are flung open to let in the fresh air, and in the darker months candles are lit and the focus is on coziness and warmth. Cut flowers are very popular—the Swedes buy more tulips per capita than anywhere else in the world. Houses and apartments are well insulated and well heated, and windows are usually triple-glazed and draft proofed.

THE RECYCLING REVOLUTION

In 2019, the sixteen-year-old Swedish climate activist Greta Thunberg addressed the UN with the memorable words "Our house is on fire." Most Swedes are, like Greta, concerned about climate change, and this has led to an increased focus on recycling and reusing. Swedish households produce about 4.5 million tons of refuse a year, which needs to be dealt with. Neighborhoods have recycling bins for newsprint, cardboard, tin cans, colored and clear glass, hard plastic, and batteries. Approximately 50 percent of this material is burned and turned into energy to heat apartment buildings and fuel buses. Many homes and apartment buildings have compost bins for food scraps.

Since 1994, Sweden has had a can and plastic bottle deposit scheme called the *pant* system. This gives you money back when you recycle. Each year the Swedes recycle 1.8 billion bottles and cans that would otherwise be thrown away.

In 2020, the Swedish government dramatically increased the tax on plastic bags, a measure that had an immediate noticeable effect.

Retro and secondhand charity shops are popular as well as reuse networks and apps where people can exchange articles with each other. In the town of Eskilstuna, a shopping mall called ReTuna is the world's first recycling mall, revolutionizing shopping in a climate-smart way. Old items are given new life through repair and upcycling. Everything sold is recycled or reused or has been organically or sustainably produced.

Contemporary Swedish kitchen.

LIVING CONDITIONS

Most of the Swedish population live in the southern part of the country, and within an hour of the main cities of Stockholm, Gothenburg, and Malmö. About half live in houses and half in apartments. All dwellings have indoor plumbing and heating. Houses tend to be heated via their own central heating system, and more than 80 percent of apartment blocks are heated by "district heating." This is an environmentally friendly system that generates the heat in large plants outside the city and distributes it through a system of insulated underground pipes into the buildings. The shift from individual oil tanks to district heating in the early 1990s is perhaps the single most important factor in explaining Sweden's reduced greenhouse gas emissions.

Thermal and solar heating systems are also becoming more common in new builds.

There are some new houses in the remote countryside, but the majority tend to be built on suburban housing estates and serviced by public transportation and other amenities. Houses usually have a driveway for parking and their own garden. Take a stroll around any suburban area and you will probably see colorful wooden houses in well-groomed neighborhoods, with trampolines in the garden and robot lawnmowers clipping the lawn.

Apartments in Sweden can be compact. This works well as around 40 percent of households are single occupancy, the highest proportion in the EU, reflecting the Swedish values of independence and self-reliance.

Most apartment buildings have communal areas, such as a shared garden with garden furniture, a barbecue area, and space to cultivate vegetables for those who are interested. Some may have party premises or bedrooms that can be rented for visitors. Older apartment buildings have a shared laundry room, while new builds tend to install washing machines and driers in each apartment. Every apartment has its own storage cage, usually in the cellar or the attic, for keeping skis, suitcases, and boxes of keepsakes. The stairways and corridors are supposed to be kept free due to fire safety, although it is not unusual for them to be cluttered with shoes, pushchairs, scooters, and kick bikes.

One unusual aspect of living in Sweden in winter is the danger of the sudden falling of long, pointed icicles and heavy masses of snow from the roofs. Building owners are required to remove these and to warn pedestrians of the potential danger by placing special signs or barricades on the sidewalks. Snow removal from the streets is excellent, and in some parts of Stockholm the sidewalks are heated.

Neighbors often communicate with each other via, usually anonymous, notes on the main entrance door or on a communal notice board. This has given rise to the *argalappen*, "the angry note," by means of which neighbors can ventilate their irritation with each other in a passive-aggressive way rather than by direct confrontation. This is so common that there is a Web site dedicated to the angry note on which people post pictures of notes from their building—www.argalappen.se.

Many apartments have balconies and, as soon as the weather permits, the residents are outside enjoying the sun. Coal-grill barbecuing on the balcony is not allowed. People generally show respect toward each other and do not stare into each other's apartments.

Don't Look!

An American visitor commented to a Swedish friend that her neighbor walked around naked without drawing the curtains. Her Swedish friend responded that the onus was on her not to look!

Swedish homes are usually very digitalized. With national broadband coverage of almost 100 percent, each household is connected and filled with various devices to entertain or make life easier.

ARCHITECTURE

Typical Swedish buildings range from characterful wooden cottages to hypermodern residences, and architecture and interior design are an interest for many Swedes. This probably isn't that surprising for the country that created IKEA.

In the older cities, a lot of nineteenth-century buildings are very well preserved. With their large stuccoed rooms, tall windows, tiled fireplaces, and high ceilings, they have elegant interiors and are very

Traditional red-painted wooden house in the countryside.

Colorful urban houses in Stockholm's lively Södermalm district.

desirable to live in. In the postwar years, a million homes were built to accommodate the growing population, and the buildings were designed in the brutal modernist style of that era. While many of these buildings have been renovated, some are in shabby condition today. There was another housing boom in the first decades of the 2000s, in which buildings were constructed from modern materials, with spacious balconies and large windows to maximize the light. New-build apartments are often open-plan, with the kitchen and living area in one large room. Award-winning architectural areas include former docklands areas such as Sjöstaden in Stockholm and Västra Hamnen in Malmö. In the 2010s, high rises became popular again, and the impact can be seen, for example, in Stockholm's changing skyline.

The Swedish countryside contains many examples of different eras of architecture. The "Decorated Farmhouses of Hälsingland" show traditional Swedish construction techniques in the wealthy farming society of the 1800s in the county of Hälsingland. Of the forty magnificent farmhouses that are open to visitors, seven are included on the UNESCO World Heritage List. Other examples of traditional architecture in Sweden are the whitewashed long houses in the county of Skåne, and the rust-red wooden cottages of Dalarna County.

FINDING A HOME

If you are moving to Sweden for a prolonged period, finding an apartment to rent can be difficult, especially in the cities. If you do manage to find one, it can be very pricey. Buying a home is also quite costly, as purchasers pay a minimum deposit of 15 percent of the value of the property. On top of this, compulsory amortizing of a part of the loan can make owning an apartment expensive. That said, most Swedes own their apartment or house. When you buy an apartment in Sweden you buy a share in a tenants' association for which you pay a monthly fee called a *månadsavgift*. Together, the residents own the building and its communal areas and the monthly fee pays for the upkeep of this. This means you must apply to the tenants' board to be approved to buy an apartment, which usually involves a credit and criminal record check. It is very unusual to be denied.

The best place to look for an apartment or house is on the Web site www.hemnet.se. Viewings are usually open, although you can sometimes book a private viewing. Homes sell quickly in the cities due to the shortage, so it is a good idea to make sure your finances are already in place so that you can make a bid. Bidding wars are common, and apartments often sell for 20–30 percent more than their asking price. If you are fortunate to win a bidding war, you will be asked to sign a contract within a couple of days. This contract is binding. The actual purchase documents are signed two to three months later when you get the keys and can move in.

The rental market in Sweden is a jungle. Local authorities and housing associations have a stock of property that they rent out. To get this type of accommodation, a so-called "firsthand lease," you register on a waiting list, and the wait can be up to twenty years in some cases! Renting "second hand" fills the gap between buying your own apartment and getting a firsthand lease. Secondhand contracts are usually insecure and short-term, and usually involve private people renting out their homes while they travel for a year or test out living with their partner. These types of rental apartments are usually furnished. Sometimes the renting is done under the radar, and in other cases via letting agencies. Some useful agencies are: www.bostadsportal.se, www.bostaddirekt.com, and www.homeq.se.

There is also a black market for the illegal sale of firsthand contracts, but the government has clamped down on this abuse of the system in recent years and the crime can attract a hefty fine or prison sentence of up to four years.

Furnishings and Appliances

Stoves and fridge-freezers are usually provided with the apartment, even when you buy it. Lighting fixtures often are not. Gas and electric costs are payable by the tenant to the utility companies, as are digital television, broadband, and Wi-Fi. Most homes do not have fixed-line telephones as the mobile network is so advanced and widespread.

Swedish electricity requires a two-pronged, round plug, so adapters are required if you come from outside the EU.

IDENTITY CARDS AND RESIDENCY

All Swedes have a personal number (*personnummer*) that is printed on an ID card or driver's license with their portrait picture. These cards are used, for example, to verify identity when seeking medical help, renting a car, registering for school, buying an apartment, or for banking. EU citizens have a right to live and work in Sweden and should apply for a Swedish personal number at the Tax Office.

If citizens from outside the EU want to visit Sweden, they may need to apply for a permit beforehand. Which permit depends on the length of stay. If for less than 90 days, they may need to apply for a visa; if more than 90 days, they need to apply for a visitor's residence permit. For more information, go to www.migrationsverket.se.

THE DAILY ROUND

The typical Swedish adult rises early, around 6:00–7:00 a.m., and, if working in an office, is usually there by 8:00 or 8:30 a.m. Some may even get up earlier to have a relaxing hour before the rest of the household awakens. If not rushing off to the gym, breakfast at home could be a smoothie, oatmeal porridge, bread or crispbread and butter, with ham, salami, cheese, and perhaps cucumber or tomato. There could be hard- or soft-boiled eggs, yogurt, sour milk, fruit, orange juice, milk, tea, or coffee.

It is usual in Sweden to eat a hot meal at lunchtime. In fact, if you want to eat more cheaply at a restaurant lunch is a good option. Classic Swedish restaurants commonly offer daily specials that include bread and butter, a salad, a main course, and a beverage. These restaurants typically serve traditional Swedish home cooking. Other restaurants offer all types of food at lunchtime, from sushi to tacos, curry to Hawaiian poke bowls. At weekends, it is popular to eat brunch.

Supper on weekdays varies depending on whether the parents are driving their children to evening

activities such as ice hockey, dance, or football.
Otherwise, families tend to eat at around 6:00 p.m. This
is usually another meal such as a pasta dish, meatballs,
or fish. After this, many Swedes may continue working,
or spend time with their children. Bedtime is around
10:30 or 11:00 p.m. on weeknights.

PARENTAL PARTNERSHIP

Because of the value placed on equality, it is not assumed
that housework is a gender-specific activity. There is
no question in Swedish households that parenting and
chores should not be shared fairly. What "fairly" means,
of course, depends on how each couple interprets it.
As a result, Swedish men participate in cooking, child
nurturing, cleaning, and laundry. Women may well be

the higher earners or be absent from home for extensive business travel. Anything else would be considered old-fashioned and obsolete. Swedish society promotes gender equality and expects both men and women to be active in the workplace, and having children should not, and does not, prevent this. Housewives are a rare breed in Sweden.

Many systems are in place to support gender equality. For example, paid parental leave is among the most generous in the world. A parent is entitled to 480 days paid parental leave per child, based on income! As we have seen, each parent has an exclusive right to 90 of those days. If they are not taken, they cannot be transferred to the other parent. Today, men take about 30 percent of all paid parental leave and this is visible when you look around the streets and parks in most Swedish towns. Groups of men with pushchairs and take-away coffees are seen everywhere and have become known as "*latte pappas.*"

Swedish employment law provides strong protection for parents returning to the workplace. This means that time off in the early years of a baby's life is not the end of a career, but rather a temporary pause. Most parents return to work in some form when the baby is eighteen months and the child then goes to one of the state subsidized nurseries. Their daily routine often involves one parent dropping off the child on the way to work, and the other leaving work early to pick the child up at the end of the day. The situation is, of course, more challenging for single-parent families. If a parent needs to take days off to care for a sick child, there is economic compensation, which is available for parents of children under twelve years. For children aged twelve to fifteen a doctor's certificate is required. This compensation is not gender-specific and can be claimed by either parent.

As there are millions of parents in Sweden there are many ways to parent. A common approach, however, is the concept of "communicative parenting." Many Swedes prefer to have dialogues with their children, rather than taking an authoritarian approach. Children are deliberately involved in many decisions and learn at an early age that their viewpoint and their voice counts. This extends from the family into the school system, where children are encouraged to express themselves. Swedish children are on first-name terms with their teachers from the very beginning.

THE SCHOOL YEARS

Education is a strong priority in Swedish society and is therefore tax-funded. Between the ages of one and five, children start attending preschool, which is heavily subsidized by the taxpayer. Preschool hours are commonly 6:00 a.m. to 6:00 p.m. School for children aged six to nineteen—from preschool class to upper secondary school—is also fully tax-funded, usually including lunches. Schools run Monday through Friday, a maximum of eight hours a day for older students and six for younger, with the exact calendar and times

established by the respective municipalities. Children between the ages of six and thirteen are also offered out-of-school care before and after school hours.

Approximately 90 percent of Swedes complete upper-secondary education. University education is also free for the individual, although students pay their own accommodation and living expenses, for which many take out a low-interest loan. Free education applies also to students from elsewhere in the EU, but not to students from outside it. There are also government-sponsored education programs aimed at, for example, retraining the unemployed, integrating non-Swedes, and supporting adults who want to complement their schooling.

CHAPTER SIX

TIME OUT

LEISURE

The Swedes have a lot of free time—a minimum five weeks' paid vacation and many public holidays. In the summer months they make as much of the outdoors as possible with picnics, sports events, or socializing al fresco at sidewalk cafés. Young people sometimes gather and drink alcohol in local parks, which can get a bit rowdy later at night. In winter, there is theater, the cinema, museums, or dining out. Brunch is a weekend treat. Throughout the year, people exercise enthusiastically and participate in sporting activities, both indoors and outdoors.

Swedes love being active outdoors all year round. In the winter they go for long walks in the crisp snow, ski along forest tracks, and skate on one of the many frozen lakes, while jogging, hiking, swimming, and picnicking are favorite ways of enjoying Sweden's long, beautiful summer days.

The pleasures of allotment life.

Winter is also a time to travel abroad to escape the cold and the dark, and the Swedes have a long reach. Popular winter destinations are the Canary Islands, the USA, and Thailand.

Many Swedes love gardening. In recent years urban farming has become a trend, with city dwellers growing vegetables in window boxes, on roof tops, and in communal courtyards. Some may also own an allotment where they can grow flowers, herbs, and vegetables. Possessing an allotment is so desirable that the waiting list can be up to twenty years in certain areas.

Beach Life

Come the summer and the Swedes hit the beaches. It is not uncommon for people to jump in as soon as the temperature rises above 59°F (15°C). You will find them bathing in the numerous lakes up and down the country, or diving from the rocky coastlines around Gothenburg and Stockholm.

There are also many sandy beaches in Sweden, some commercialized and others pristine and undisturbed. Popular beaches include Tofta on the island of Gotland, Böda Sand on the island of Öland, Tylösand in county Halland, and Pite Havsbad in Piteå in Swedish Lapland. Sweden's highest water temperatures are often recorded at Pite Havsbad, which is hard to believe given its northerly location. Sandhammaren in the very south of the country has won several awards for being Sweden's best beach, because of its dunes and its long stretch of fine white sand. This area is also the scene of many a

Summer on the beach at Åhus on Skåne County's east coast.

grizzly crime in the internationally renowned TV thriller series about Inspector Kurt Wallander.

Further along the coast from Sandhammaren is the village of Kåseberga. On a hilltop overlooking the village, you will find Ale's Stones (Ales stenar). This is an early iron-age monument consisting of 59 massive boulders arranged in a 220-foot-long (67 meters) outline of a ship, with a magnificent view over the Baltic Sea. It is believed to have been erected around 1,400 years ago but, to this day, its purpose remains a mystery.

Theme Parks

There are permanent theme parks in Stockholm (Gröna Lund) and Gothenburg (Liseberg). They feature beer gardens, concert areas, restaurants, and hair-raising rides. Other theme parks include Skara Sommarland in Skara, Astrid Lindgren's World in Småland, and Furuviksparken in Gävle. Kolmården Wildlife Park, about an hour south of Stockholm, is one of the most popular tourist destinations in the Nordic countries.

Gaming

Gaming and e-sports are popular in Sweden, perhaps because of the long dark winters. Sweden produces DreamHack, the world's largest digital festival, which attracts more than 300,000 gaming and e-sports enthusiasts annually. Several successful games such as Minecraft, Battlefield, and Candy Crush Saga were developed in Sweden. Swedish gamer PewDiPie has 107 million devoted YouTube subscribers.

Popular Culture

During the coldest months of the year, the Swedes spend a lot of time watching television. Other than series and films, popular programs are sports events, reality programs, quizzes, and music shows. "Melodifestivalen" is the most popular TV program in Sweden. This is a music competition that is broadcast on six Saturdays in February and March every year, where the Swedish population selects the song that will represent Sweden at the international Eurovision Song Contest in May. "Melodifestivalen" has been broadcast almost every year since 1959, and today almost half the Swedish population tunes in to watch the final.

THE GREAT OUTDOORS

Many Swedes are inseparable from nature, which brings them inner peace and harmony. Hiking, walking in the woods, and berry picking are all favorite pastimes. Many towns maintain trails for cross-country skiing, jogging, walking, running, cycling, and horseback riding. In national parks in the far north, such as Sarek, the Swedish Tourist Foundation maintains trailside huts where hikers can stay for a nominal fee. As we have seen, by law the "Right t Roam" allows the Swedes nearly unlimited access to any land or waterfront area, whether for mushrooming in the spring and fall, or for boating among the 25,000 islands in the Swedish archipelago. Sweden is also a fisherman's paradise, with

Berry picking in the forests of northern Sweden.

more than 96,000 lakes and a national border that is mainly coastline.

As a way to get back to nature, around 1.8 million people own a summer cottage (*sommarstuga*). This is often very simple, which is part of the charm, and some even have primitive outside toilets.

SPORTY SWEDES

The Swedes are in general a sports-loving nation—more than 3.1 million of them are registered in some sort of sports club or society.

The two most widely followed spectator sports are ice hockey in winter and football (soccer) in summer. Other popular sports include golf, handball, *innebandy*

Cross-country skiing.

(floorball), hunting, fishing, tennis, ice-skating, biking, kayaking, and sailing. Skiing is in the Swedish DNA, with cross-country and downhill skiing being extremely popular. It seems that as soon as a child can stand, they are put onto a pair of skis. Popular ski resorts are Åre and Sälen. *Bandy*, a sport similar to ice hockey, is unique to Sweden, and is sometimes called winter's football. *Innebandy*, the indoor version of this, was invented as recently as the late 1960s.

Many Swedes enjoy exercising with a goal in mind and there are many organized races throughout the year:

- Göteborgsvarvet—a half marathon road running competition in Gothenburg, this is the largest annual running competition in the world in terms of its 64,500 entries.

Yachts in the Round Gotland Race, a two-day regatta in the southern Baltic.

- Stockholm marathon—the largest marathon in Sweden with around 18,000 participants, it takes place in June every year.
- The Midnight Race—usually held in August, this 6.2-mile (10-kilometer) race around the island of Södermalm is very popular. There are 16,000 runners and a carnival atmosphere. It's also held in Stockholm in August and in Gothenburg and Malmö in September.
- The Vasaloppet in Mora—held on the first Sunday in March, this is the world's oldest cross-country ski race, attracting 16,000 participants who ski the grueling 56 miles (90 kilometers).

- Tjejmilen—this is a race for women only in Stockholm, which takes place in late August.
- Tough Viking—the largest and most brutal obstacle race in the Nordics takes place in Stockholm in October.
- The Stockholm Santa Run in December is a jolly charity event in which the participants all dress up as Santa.

Other smaller events are also organized in other parts of the country.

The Swedish Classic Circuit

The Swedish classic circuit, *en svensk klassiker*, is a diploma awarded to those who have finished long-distance endurance races in four challenging disciplines during a twelve-month period. These races are among the longest, oldest, and most exhausting in the world. The Swedish Classic Circuit award began in 1972, and since then completing the circuit has become a rite of passage for sporty Swedes. Thousands of people take part in all four races each year. In 2014, the first wheelchair user completed the circuit. See https://ensvenskklassiker.se/en/. The races include:

- Engelbrektsloppet—37 miles (60 km) on skis.
- Vasaloppet—50 miles (80 km) on skis.
- Vättenrundan—186.4 miles (300 km) on a bike.
- Vansbrosimmet—9,843 feet (3,000 m) swimming in a cold, dark, fast river, against the current.
- Lindingöloppet—18.6 miles (30 km) running in hilly, natural terrain.

Non-violence. Bronze sculpture by Carl Fredrik Reuterswärd in Malmö.

THE CULTURAL SCENE

Museums

The many state-owned museums in Sweden are free,
but you will have to pay to enter privately owned
establishments. Stockholm is home to the majority
of museums including the Vasa Museum, the Royal
Palace Museum, the Royal Treasury, the Abba Museum,
the Viking Museum, the Museum of Modern Art,
the Photography Museum (Fotografiska), children's
author Astrid Lindgren's Junibacken, and the National
Museum. To find a museum in the capital, go to www.
visitstockholm.com. In Gothenburg you will find the
Volvo Museum, the natural science center Universeum,
and the aviation museum Aeroseum. Malmö is home to
the "Disgusting Food Museum" and the Form Design

Entrance to the Universeum in Gothenburg.

Center, and just a twenty-minute train ride across
the sea takes you to the museums of neighboring
Copenhagen. The tiniest museum in Sweden, at just
under 183 square feet (17 square meters), is a tribute
to a comedy duo called Hasse and Tage, which can be
found in the rural village of Tomelilla in Skåne.

Castles, Palaces, and Stately Homes

The Swedish countryside is populated with castles,
palaces, and stately homes. Some are privately owned
and many are open to the public. You will find stunning
town-center castles in Örebro, Vadstena, and Kalmar.
On the edge of magical lakesides you will discover
castles such as Gripsholm, Skokloster, and Läckö,
all reflecting a time in Swedish history of power
struggle and war. Just outside Stockholm, the Palace

Vadstena Castle, first built in 1545 and continously reconstructed until 1620.

of Drottningholm, where the King and Queen reside, is well worth a visit. The southern region of Skåne has a lot of castles and grand homes. For more information go to www.visitskane.com/culture-history/castles-strongholds.

Other houses that are open to visitors include the homes of artists, writers, and gentry. In Stockholm you can visit the home of the sculptor Carl Milles and the royal painter Prince Eugene, and in Dalarna the homes of painters Anders Zorn and Carl Larsson are open to the public. In Värmland you can visit Sunnborn, the home of author Selma Lagerlöf, and by Lake Vättern the feminist writer Ellen Key's home is open for viewing. The palatial home of the Hallwyl family in Stockholm gives a fascinating glimpse into the life of a wealthy nineteenth-century industrialist. On Fjällgatan in Stockholm, overlooking the harbor, Anna Lindhagen's museum (Stigbergets Borgarum) is a small museum in the apartment of a middle-class family from the mid 1800s.

The Performing Arts

Stockholm, Gothenburg, and Malmö have thriving performing arts scenes. Dansens Hus in Stockholm is Sweden's largest venue for domestic and international contemporary dance and performance art. Also in Stockholm, there are many large institutions such as Dramaten (the Royal Dramatic Theater), Statsteatern (City Theater, based in Kulturhuset—the House of Culture), and the Royal Opera. Theatrical performances are almost exclusively in Swedish. Many smaller

The Art Nouveau building of the Royal Dramatic Theater in Stockholm.

independent theaters exist, which sometimes put on performances in other languages. The Playhouse Theater in central Stockholm stages contemporary off-Broadway productions translated into Swedish. Musical theater is very popular in Sweden, with Swedish-language versions of modern classics such as *Cabaret*, *The Book of Mormon*, and *The Sound of Music*.

Gothenburg and Malmö have reputable opera companies and several theaters. The northern town of Rättvik has an impressive concert and opera stage—built in the remains of a huge quarry—and on the island of Gotland performances are staged during the summer months inside the ruins of various churches and fortresses.

Government subsidies enable ordinary people to attend quality performances at half the price of New York tickets. Dress can range from elegant to casual.

Two popular sites for booking tickets are www. showtic.se and www.ticketmaster.se.

Live Music

For classical music, Stockholm's historic Konserthus—site of the Nobel Prize ceremonies—is home to the Royal Philharmonic Orchestra. The city's contemporary Berwaldshallen concert house is the home of Sweden's Radio Symphony Orchestra. Most of the churches around the country hold regular concerts showcasing musicians and choral groups.

Jazz and blues are popular in Sweden and can be seen live in venues such as Nalen and Fasching in Stockholm.

Sweden has several large arenas in its main cities, the largest being Friends Arena, which opened in 2012 and has a capacity of 75,000. Before 2012, Stockholm's largest arena was Ericsson Globe, which takes up to 16,000 people and is still today the largest hemispherical building on earth. Other large arenas are Tele2 Arena in Stockholm and Ullevi in Gothenburg, both with a capacity of 40,000. With these relatively large venues, Sweden attracts international artists, with rap artist Eminem holding the record for the largest audience in 2020. A popular site to buy concert tickets is www.livenation.se.

In the summer months, Sweden hosts many outdoor festivals, such as Summerburst in Gothenburg and the Sweden Rock Festival in Blekinge, both in June. In July, Lollapalooza takes over in Stockholm, and Way Out West takes place in Gothenburg in August. Also in August is the Stockholm Pride Festival, Scandinavia's largest gay pride celebration, with 60,000 people participating in the parade. For more information about festivals, go to: www.swedenfestivals.com.

Swedish Dance Band Culture

A very popular and distinctly Swedish form of entertainment is "dance band music," a musical genre that non-Swedes may find baffling, even bizarre. It is a form of live band music, danced to in pairs, which is influenced by jitterbug, swing, schlager (catchy pop), and country music. It has its roots in the 1950s and '60s, when people would dance in the open air to live bands in their local park. Traditionally, the performers wear highly extravagant matched outfits in spandex and glitter. Since 1986, every year in July a dance band festival has been held in the small town of Malung, attracting around 50,000 dance-hungry Swedes.

RESTAURANTS, FOOD, AND DRINK

In 2020 there were thirteen restaurants in Sweden with at least one star in the Michelin guide, most of them in Stockholm. Many Swedes love dining out and there is a great variety of international cuisines and eateries. All restaurants also offer take-out food and home delivery services can be booked via the apps of Uber Eats, Wolt, and Foodora. Whatever food takes your fancy, you can usually find it, and it is almost always good quality. The *White Guide* lists the 800 best restaurants in the country. It can be read in paper, app, or Web form: www.whiteguide.se. TripAdvisor and Yelp are also good ways to identify restaurants.

There are many restaurants offering classic Swedish cuisine. Some choose to present the food traditionally, while others may put a modern, fusion twist on it.

Some Classic Swedish Dishes
Gravadlax—cured salmon served with sauce and potatoes.
Inlagd sill—pickled herring served with boiled potatoes and washed down with snaps.

Clockwise: Fillet of herring with pepper, rosemary, onion and lime; meatballs with cream sauce and parsley; sandwiches with shrimps and caviar; potato pancake with lingonberries and syrup.

Jansson's Temptation—a gratin of potato, cream, and anchovies.

Meatballs and lingonberry preserve.

Raggmunk—crispy potato pancake, often served with ham.

Renskav—thinly-sliced reindeer.

Råraka—thin potato fritter, similar to hash browns.

Stekt strömming—fried herring served with potato puree and melted butter.

Toast Skagen—shrimps and mayonnaise on toasted bread.

The *Smörgåsbord*

The Swedish *smörgåsbord* sounds exotic but is basically a self-service buffet of various dishes. In homes, it is common to have a *smörgåsbord* at Christmas, Easter, on birthdays and other celebrations. In restaurants, the Christmas buffet season runs through December. It is extremely easy to overindulge at a *smörgåsbord*, so the trick is to take small amounts and to start with cold dishes, then move onto warm before hitting the desserts. You can return to a *smörgåsbord* as many times as you want, taking a fresh clean plate every time.

Ice Cream Renaissance

The average Swede is said to lick their way through a massive 28½ pints (13½ liters) of ice cream per year, making it an EU record. In recent years, there has been an ice cream revival in Sweden and lots of organic artisan ice cream bars and gelaterias have popped up. Traditional tastes are mixed in with classic Swedish flavors such as dill, pine, and cloudberry. In Stockholm, ice cream places worth a visit are La Gelateria Sofo, Snö, Stikki Nikki, and King Scoopa.

Eating Out

It is relatively expensive to dine out at restaurants in the evenings, but despite this it can be difficult to get a table, so book in advance if possible. Booking Web sites include www.thefork.se and www.bokabord.se.

Restaurant food is less expensive at lunchtime, between 11:00 a.m. and 14:00 p.m., and cheap meals can be had at fast-food restaurants and kiosks selling hot dogs, burgers, and kebabs. In the large cities, an app called Karma minimizes food waste by helping consumers find delicious surplus food from restaurants, cafés, and grocery stores to enjoy at half the regular price: www.karma.life. When eating out with Swedes, check how the bill will be settled— whether split equally among everybody or by paying only for what you've had. This differs from group to group.

A word to the wise: "doggie-bag" devotees, beware! The Swedes consider it rather déclassé to ask for a doggie bag.

No Smoking Sweden

In health-conscious Sweden around 10 percent of the population smoke, and the number continues to decline. All restaurants are smoke free and, since 2019, this even applies to the outside seating areas and other public areas. If you want to smoke, you'll have to walk some distance away from the restaurant to enjoy your cigarette. It is also illegal to smoke in a doorway to a building, on train platforms, at bus stops, taxi zones, ticketing areas, sports facilities, and playgrounds.

Waiters, Service, and Tipping

Waiting staff speak fluent English and are usually helpful. A service charge is almost always included in the bill but tipping up to 10 percent is common practice, depending on how satisfied you are with the service. Swedes do not usually tip at lunchtime. The waiters are generally well paid and do not rely on tips.

Drinking

The average Swede drinks almost 21 US pints (10 liters) of pure alcohol per year, and men drink more than women. Wine is the most popular alcoholic drink, followed by beer, and then spirits. Vodka is by far the most popular spirit, followed by whiskey and Jägermeister, which is drunk like a shot. Around Christmas and Midsummer, sales of *snaps* and aquavit rocket. Because of the rigid licensing laws, bars and nightclubs have to keep drunk people under strict control. This means you may be asked to leave, even if you do not feel too drunk yourself. If this happens, simply accept your fate and leave graciously.

Swedes are among the highest per capita consumers of coffee in the world. Many adult Swedes drink milk, and plant-based "milk" drinks from almond, oats, and cashew nuts are rapidly growing in popularity. Carbonated soft drinks and concentrates are often included in the price of lunch at restaurants.

Beer Culture

Brewing and beer drinking in Sweden is a tradition that goes back centuries. In recent years, an interest in craft beer has exploded and today the main cities have a vibrant beer scene. Although expensive, the beers are top quality, and there is a wide range of brewery bars to choose from, both international and local. Scottish brewery Brewdog has bars in Stockholm, Gothenburg, and Malmö. In the docklands area of Sjöstan, located in a former lighthouse factory, lies an enormous brewery called Nya Carnegie Bryggeriet. Here, you can grab a beer, have some food, and go on a brewery tour.

Farther afield, you can head to the picturesque island of Fjäderholmarna and visit their brewery and brew pub. Hop on a ferry from central Stockholm, and within twenty minutes you are there, trying out their various beers with some food, or going on a tour of the brewery.

For a wide variety of beers, head to one of Stockholm's many specialist pubs. Kvarnen, established in 1908, is an enormous beer hall and a glimpse of Sweden's past. Other recommended pubs are The Flying Dog, Pressklubben, Sjatte Tunnan, The Queen's Head, Akkurat, and Pubologi. Check out their Web sites for information about their area of expertise.

Independent craft breweries in Gothenburg include Oceanbryggeriet, and Göteborgs Nya Bryggeri. Gothenburg also hosts several beer festivals each year, including the Gothenburg Brewers Guild Beer Festival.

For more information on the flourishing craft beer scene and events in Sweden, check out www.cohops.se.

VISITOR ATTRACTIONS

Visited by approximately one million visitors a year, the Vasa Museum in Stockholm houses the pride of the Swedish Imperial fleet, the Vasa battleship. She sank on her maiden voyage in 1628 and was salvaged in 1961 from the depths of Stockholm's harbor. Other attractions in Stockholm include Skansen open-air museum, the Royal Palace, and the Abba Museum. Travel further north and you will find the amazing Ice Hotel above the Arctic circle. Alternatively, travel east to the romantic medieval town of Visby on the island of Gotland, or south to the imposing Romanesque cathedral in the city of Lund. An excellent way to experience Sweden is by boat, so take one of the sightseeing boats and view the townscapes from the water. In Stockholm, it is a treat to take a ferry out into the archipelago and see the thousands of islands outside the capital city. You can also book lunch on the ferries, which adds to the romance of the experience.

UNESCO World Heritage Sites

Sweden has fifteen official World Heritage Sites, which are all open to visitors. For more information, go to www.visitsweden.com. Here is a selection:

In and around Stockholm

The Woodland Cemetery (Skogskyrkogården)—an amazing graveyard with graves positioned in and among the trees.

View over the town center of Visby on the island of Gotland.

The Royal Domain of Drottningholm—the Royal family residence, with the Royal Palace, period gardens, a Chinese Pavilion, and the only surviving eighteenth-century theater in the world with the original machinery and sets preserved. The theater is still in use.

The Viking Settlement of Birka, just over 18.6 miles (30 km) outside the capital city on the island of Björkö. It is one of the most complete examples of a Viking trading settlement of the eighth to tenth centuries and is reachable by boat from Stockholm.

To the East
In the Baltic Sea, to the east of Sweden, lie the two main islands of Gotland and Öland. Both islands have permanent populations and are very popular summer holiday destinations for Swedes.

The Hanseatic Town of Visby

The island of Gotland has fascinating flora and fauna. Its main town, Visby, dates to the twelfth century and is a well-preserved Hanseatic town with a number of ruins and a medieval ring wall. If you have the time, jump on a ferry and, within a couple of hours from the mainland, you are thrown straight back into the Middle Ages. To the north of Gotland, lies the island of Fårö—a mystical, barren place that was the residence of film director Ingemar Bergman. Many of his productions were filmed here and, every year in June, Bergman Week is hosted on the island.

Agricultural Landscape of Southern Öland

People have been living on Öland for 5,000 years, and have long adapted their way of life to this windy island. It has a vast limestone plateau that is rich in biodiversity. The Swedish Royal family have their summer residence, Solliden, here. Öland can be reached from Kalmar on the mainland by a 3.7 mile (6 km) bridge.

To the North
The High Coast/Kvarken Archipelago

The High Coast is situated on one side of the Gulf of Bothnia in the north of the Baltic Sea, opposite the Finnish Kvarken Archipelago. The breathtaking landscape is the result of the last Ice Age, which created the world's highest coastline, as well as thousands of low-lying islands, shallow bays, and fields of boulders.

To the South
The Naval Port of Karlskrona

Founded in 1679 by King Karl XI, this naval base and port city is exceptionally well-preserved and contains one of the few dockyards in the world where it is still possible to see fortifications, maritime defensive installations, and shipyards designed for the construction of warships. Karlskrona itself is a Baroque gem, with wonderful squares, churches, and monuments, including the Church of the Holy Trinity, the Fredrik Church, and Karlskrona Rådhus—the old city hall.

To the West
The Rock Carvings at Tanum

About 90 minutes drive north of Gothenburg is the province of Bohuslän, a popular summer holiday

Prehistoric rock carving depicting men in boats at Tanum.

destination on Sweden's west coast. Bohuslän is distinguished by its tidal salty sea (unlike the more brackish Baltic), its stunning rocky coastline with about 3,000 islands, and 1,500 rock carving sites. The carvings in Tanum, depicting people, animals, and objects, are excellent examples of Nordic Bronze Age art. For more information, go to www.visitsweden.se, www.sweden.com, or www.visitstockholm.com.

SHOPPING

Sweden is a consumerist society and there is a great deal of choice on the shopping front. Well-known clothing chains such as H&M and Zara can be found

Shopping in Stockholm's pedestrianized Drottninggatan Street (Queen Street).

in most towns. Downtown Stockholm, Gothenburg, and Malmö have thriving city centers, despite competition from the enormous shopping malls in the suburbs. Scandinavia's largest shopping mall, the Mall of Scandinavia, was opened in the Stockholm suburb of Solna in 2015.

Being the home of IKEA, Sweden has twenty stores from above the Arctic Circle to the southernmost tip of the country. Another large store, which has something of a cult status in Sweden, is called Gekås. Situated in Ullared, this megastore is a mecca for those looking for cheap items. It is so popular that a reality TV show is filmed there.

Typically, Swedish materials for clothing, gift-wrapping, or interior design reflect nature. These include cotton, linen, or wool fibers; simple bows and ribbons on plain paper; and colors that exist in a natural state, like berry red or dark evergreen. Christmas tree ornaments are often made of straw and wood.

For food shopping, Sweden has two major chains, ICA and Coop. These exist in smaller versions in downtown districts and in megastore format on industrial estates. There are smaller specialist food stores and markets in the main cities, such as on Hötorget in Stockholm and Möllevången in Malmö. Food is relatively expensive in Sweden, with VAT at 12 percent. A Farmers' Market takes place on fall and spring Saturdays in the Södermalm district of Stockholm, where you can buy fresh produce straight from the farm. It is not cheap, but it is organic.

Buying Alcohol

Alcohol can be bought in bars and restaurants assuming you are over eighteen years of age. Wines, spirits, and strong beer can only be purchased at state-owned alcohol stores called Systembolaget. You must be over twenty years old to buy alcohol in Systembolaget. These have restricted opening hours, usually 10:00 a.m. to 7:00 p.m. on weekdays and 10:00 a.m. to 3:00 p.m. on Saturdays. They are closed on Sundays. Low alcohol beer, known as *folköl* can be bought at supermarkets.

Systembolaget is one of the world's largest single importers of alcohol, and as such has a very sophisticated and varied selection of wines. Many Swedes are interested in wine-tasting and the staff at in the stores are highly trained in helping customers select the right wine to match the evening's dinner. Systembolaget is a state monopoly and is designed to preserve public health and reduce crime by limiting access to alcohol.

Shopping Hours

Most shops in the large cities are open from 10:00 a.m. to 6:00 p.m. every day of the week. In smaller towns, shops may close as early as 3.00 p.m. on Saturdays and be closed on Sundays. Shopping malls and supermarkets are often open until 10:00 p.m. Some shops may be closed on Midsummer's Day. Since times can vary across the country, check the store's Web site to be sure.

SOME USEFUL SHOPS

Konditori Bakery and coffee shop

Apoteket Pharmacy (sells both prescription medicines and over-the-counter health aids)

Matäffar Supermarket

Saluhall Food hall. Marketplace with various specialty shops, such as butcher, bakery, coffee and tea boutiques, fresh fish shop, and so on, all under one roof

Kemtvätt Dry cleaners

Systembolaget Alcohol store

Online Shopping

More than 70 percent of Swedish people regularly shop online, mostly for electronics, fashion, and groceries, making them the largest e-commerce users in Scandinavia. Popular Web sites are:

Ikea.com—furniture

Netonnet.se—electronics

Elgiganten.se—electronics and household goods

Mathem.se—groceries

Zalando.se—fashion

BANKS AND CURRENCY EXCHANGE

Most Swedes do their banking online today and this has led to the closing of bank branches up and down the country. For the banks that still exist, opening times can vary but they tend to be open on weekdays from 9:00 a.m. till 4:00 p.m. They are usually closed at weekends, on national holidays, and the day before a national holiday.

Cashless Society

If you bring cash to Sweden, you may have a lot left in your pocket when you leave. Sweden is swiftly moving toward a cashless society and, in fact, only about 20 percent of Swedes carry cash. Many shops, restaurants, and cafés accept credit cards only. Supermarkets accept cash. Commonly accepted cards are Visa and Mastercard. American Express and Diners Club have a more limited reach. Since 2012, people with a bank account in Sweden can also pay with Swish—a mobile payment system allowing the simple transfer of funds via a cell phone. This is particularly useful in restaurants when, instead of splitting the bill with several cards, one person pays the whole bill and everybody else swishes their share of the bill to him or her. A very practical, and quick, solution.

Most taxi companies take cash, credit card, or prepaid trips via their apps.

It might be good to have a small amount of cash available as a backup. This can be drawn from an ATM but be aware that there will probably be a charge. If you are exchanging money, your best bet cost-wise is a bureau de change rather than a bank or hotel. The Swedish currency is the krona (plural kronor), or the crown, and is written SEK.

SHOPPING TIPS FOR TOURISTS

Hipster Heaven

Swedish towns and cities have a typical downtown where you will find most of the major shops. If you prefer wandering around less commercialized areas, then the main cities have neighborhoods that offer an interesting alternative. These areas are fashionable and buzzing with quirky independent shops, interesting restaurants, and artisan bakeries and coffee houses. In Stockholm, head to the hip Södermalm neighborhood, especially the areas around Nytorget and Mariatorget. In Gothenburg, go to the cobbled streets of Haga, and in Malmö, go to arty Möllan.

Making Your Trip Cheaper

Standard sales tax—VAT, called *moms* in Sweden—is 25 percent on most goods and services. On food it is 12 percent and it is 6 percent on, for example newspapers, books, cultural events, taxis, bus, plane, or train. Tourists from non-EU countries are entitled to a refund on sales tax. Sweden's refund rate ranges from 8.3 percent to 19 percent of the purchase price, with a minimum purchase amount of 200 SEK per receipt. For information on how to do this, go to www.globalblue.com.

Buying Swedish

If you would like to buy something typically Swedish, focus on design, crystal ware, handicrafts, and food.

Classic Swedish design prioritizes functionality, beauty, simplicity, and sustainability, and is typically showcased in furniture, textiles, and interior objects. The best Stockholm stores profiling modern and classic Swedish design are Svensk Tenn and Nordiska Galleriet. The trendy design store Designtorget can be found in Stockholm, Gothenburg, Malmö, and Uppsala.

Sweden is world-famous for its crystal. Crystal vases, bowls, and candle holders can be found in design stores and department stores. If you are interested in the production process itself, take a trip to the forested southern region of Småland where you can visit the various factories and studios and see master craftsmen at work.

The most Swedish of all handicrafts is the "Dala horse." Originating in the Dalarna region, this carved, painted wooden horse comes in different sizes and colors, although red is traditional. Dala horses can be bought at most tourist shops, department stores, and airport shops, or direct from the horse's mouth, so to speak, at the factory in Nusnäs.

Swedish food specialties include preserves made from lingonberry and cloudberry. Cured reindeer meat and national cheeses such as Västerbottensost are also popular. A typical Swedish candy is called *bilar* (cars). Alcohol includes Absolut Vodka, various types of *snaps*, and mulled wine (*glögg*) at Christmas. To many a traveler's surprise, alcohol cannot be bought at the airport stores unless your destination is outside the EU. If you are traveling within the EU, make sure to visit the Systembolaget before you leave and pack the bottles tightly into your check-in luggage.

While sales go on throughout the year in Sweden, a typical period is from Boxing Day until the end of January. The word for sale is *Realisation*, or REA for short.

Ask Before You Buy
There is no law in Sweden that gives consumers the right to "open purchase" (*öppet köp*). Each shop can decide for itself whether or not to offer customers the possibility of returning items bought. This means that, for example, some may offer thirty days' right to return, some may only offer a credit note and not your money back, and others may offer no return right at all. Since this is unpredictable, ask before purchasing what the shop's policy is.

CHAPTER SEVEN

TRAVEL, HEALTH, & SAFETY

Transportation in Sweden is well-organized, safe, and hassle free. Since the country is so large, for long distances people usually travel by air or by train. Flights and trains are very efficient, clean, comfortable, and smoke-free. Domestic flights serve the entire country from north to south, and tickets can be bought via www.sas.se and www.braa.se.

Sweden has an excellent, but relatively expensive, rail network. Long-distance trains have "silent carriages," where speaking to each other or on the phone is not allowed. This is in order to improve the quality and comfort of the journey. To buy intercity train tickets, go to www.sj.se.

Coaches or buses connect many of the smaller towns and villages and are usually cheaper than trains. To buy tickets, go to www.flixbus.se.

Local transportation in Sweden's towns and cities varies according to the size of the population. For example, in Gothenburg there is an extensive

Road running along the shore of Torneträsk Lake, north of the Arctic Circle.

streetcar network, and in Stockholm there is a subway system. In most towns and cities, the car is the most common way of covering longer distances.

DRIVING IN SWEDEN

Rules of the Road

Despite the size of the country, driving is very popular. Swedish motorways are mostly toll-free. They may have three lanes—one lane each for opposing traffic, and a shared middle lane for overtaking. Some of the larger highways have four or six lanes. Secondary roads may have only one lane each way, with no apparent passing lane. In this case, cars being overtaken should pull over to the breakdown lane to enable a faster car to pass.

Roads leading into Stockholm and Gothenburg are subject to a congestion charge. Cameras automatically read your car's number plate as you drive through and charge the licence holder. If your car is not registered in Sweden, the authorities have a notification partner to identify non-Swedish vehicles and invoice the owners. There is also a charge when crossing the Öresund Bridge to Denmark.

On highways the speed limit is usually 68 mph (110 kmph); 75 mph (120 kmph) is only set on the best, safest, and straightest roads. Other speed limits are 56 mph (90 kmph) on secondary roads and 31–43 mph (50–70 kmph) in built-up areas. Outside schools and other protected areas, the limit is often 19 mph (30 kmph). The speed limits are indicated on signs with a yellow background. There are no "end of speed limit" signs, in contrast to most other countries in Europe. On many roads there are speed cameras to keep control of the traffic.

Carpooling and Carsharing

The usual car rental companies are found in Sweden as well as companies that operate carpools and carsharing services. Aimo and Sunfleet have their own fleets of cars, while SnappCar and Ridebite are carpooling apps. Visit their respective home pages for more information on the services and pricing.

DRIVING TIPS

- The use of seat belts is mandatory for drivers and all passengers.
- Young children must be in car seats. Children aged 0-4 should be in rear-facing car seats. Children up to 4 feet (135 cm) in height must use car seats or booster seats.
- Technically it is illegal to use cell phones when driving, but this only applies if it affects your driving negatively.
- Your car must be fitted with winter tires from December 1 to March 31. You should change to summer tires after this period. Driving with studded tires during the period April 16 to September 30 can also lead to fines unless winter conditions prevail. On certain streets, driving with studded tires is forbidden.
- There are plenty of car parks in inner city areas. Some charge you as you are leaving. The price is generally between 85 and 120 SEK per hour on weekdays. The daily (24 h) charge at a city car park is usually in the vicinity of 300 SEK.
- If you drive an electric car, check out www.uppladdning.nu to find parking bays with charging stations.
- If you park in designated street parking bays, pay attention to the signs. In most places

where street parking is allowed there are signs at the entrance to each neighborhood. Streets may be closed for parking one day a week so that they can be cleaned. Parking fines can be up to an eye-watering 1,000 SEK. Street parking meters charge by the hour; most take VISA and MasterCard.

- You must park at least 11 yards (10 meters) away from a pedestrian crossing.
- In the winter months, if you go into a skid on black ice, steer in the direction of the skid and avoid using your brakes.
- When parking overnight in the wintertime, pull your wiper blades out at right angles from the windshield to keep them from freezing onto it.
- Beware of elk, deer, and reindeer, especially at dawn and dusk, when driving through wooded areas. If you hit a cloven-hoofed animal, it is mandatory to report the accident to the police.

Penalties

You do not want to get caught speeding or otherwise driving recklessly in Sweden! Fines range from 2,000 to 4,000 SEK. The police can immediately confiscate your driver's license if they suspect you of a traffic violation such as speeding or drunk driving. Your license is then sent to the Swedish Transportation Agency who decide if it should be returned or revoked. If there are any doubts about your sobriety, it will be revoked or you will be required to install a costly alcohol lock in your car.

In certain circumstances the driver may be allowed to continue driving after the installation of an alcohol lock in their car. The limit for drunk driving is 0.10 milligrams of alcohol per liter of exhaled air. Drunk driving is punishable by steep fines or a prison sentence of up to six months. The limit for aggravated drunk driving is 0.50 milligrams of alcohol per liter of exhaled air, and the driver can be sentenced to prison for up to two years. So, if you plan to drink, take a cab home.

Driver's Licenses

If you are not a registered resident in Sweden, there is no limit on how long you can drive using your foreign license. If you have a foreign driver's license issued in a country within the EEA, Switzerland, or Japan, you may continue driving as long as the license is valid. However, if you are resident in Sweden a foreign license issued in a country outside the EEA is only valid for a year.

You must carry your license with you when you drive. The driver's license must have a photograph of you on it. If it does not, you should have a valid ID document with you bearing your photo. If your driver's license has not been issued in English, German, or French, the police may require you to have a certified translation of it. An international driver's license is a certified translation that can be used for this purpose.

If you are contemplating acquiring a Swedish license, be aware that driving lessons in Sweden are expensive, and the road test includes a test of driving on ice.

TRAINS, BUSES, AND THE SUBWAY

Local public transportation is a comfortable and efficient and is used by everybody in Swedish society. The major cities have well-developed bus networks, as well as streetcar (tram) services. Stockholm also has a very good commuter train that serves the suburbs from the city center, and a high-speed train runs from Arlanda Airport to the central railway station.

Streetcars in central Stockholm.

Stockholm is the only city in Sweden to have a subway, the Tunnelbana, which is the fastest way to get around town. The Tunnelbana is full of artwork and is sometimes referred to as the "world's longest art gallery." The service is efficient and the carriages are clean.

Stockholm Public Transport, "SL," is responsible for buses, underground trains, commuter trains, streetcars, and certain ferry lines in Greater Stockholm. Tickets for any of these can be purchased at SL Centers, subway ticket machines, newsstands, or via the SL app. You can also buy tickets by blipping your debit card on the automatic barrier or when you board the bus. Cash is not accepted on board buses in Stockholm. There are

The T-Centralen station is at the heart of Stockholm's metro system.

regular spot checks carried out by ticket inspectors and failure to produce a valid ticket on demand during a check will result in a fine of 1,200 SEK.

A single ticket is valid for 75 minutes and costs 50 SEK (38 SEK if you use a prepaid SL Card instead) and you can travel as many times as you want within the time limit. It is also possible to buy 24-hours, 72-hours, and 30-day tickets. A person with a pushchair rides free on any of Stockholm's buses.

TAXIS

Taxis are quite expensive. You can book a cab by phone or by the company's app—Taxi Kurir, Taxi Stockholm, Taxi Goteborg, and Taxi Malmö. When you book via an app you usually get a fixed price and can prepay. To pick up from the street, simply hail a passing cab or go to a taxi rank. Available cabs have an illuminated sign on the roof. The tip is included in the fare. In Stockholm, fixed fares to and from the airport cost around 350 SEK. Avoid taking unmarked cabs as the final charge can be extortionate.

A cheaper alternative to taxis are the car service companies Uber and Volt, which can be both booked via their apps. Unlike the official taxis, their fares do not include a service charge. If you want to tip the driver the custom is to add a few kronor to the fare so it reaches the nearest round number and makes it easier for the driver to give you change.

CROSSING THE ROAD

Although jaywalking is not illegal in Sweden, most Swedes cross the road at the designated pedestrian crossings. Drivers must stop for people on the crossing, even if there is no traffic light. To cross the road, hit the button and wait for the green man. On some crossings the green indicator is female, and during Pride Week it depicts a same-sex couple holding hands. If there is no light, the pedestrian has right of way. Nevertheless, to avoid accidents do not lunge into the street but take a tentative step onto the crossing and pay attention to the oncoming traffic. Cyclists do not have right of way on a pedestrian crossing.

The best way of exploring the city centers is still on foot, or by bike or electric scooter

SCOOTING AROUND

Cycling is a popular way to get around in the main cities, which have numerous cycle lanes. Helmets are a legal requirement for children under fifteen. An alternative to the cycle is the electric scooter, which can be rented by the minute. Some scooter companies also offer day, weekly, and monthly passes. These are a great way to get around independently and usually have a top speed of 12.4 miles per hour (20 kmph). It is not a legal requirement to wear a helmet, but it is recommended. You pick a scooter up where the previous user left it,

Scooting over the cobblestones in Lund.

parked on street corners, against walls, and even in the middle of the sidewalk. Download the app, register your credit card, and off you go. Popular scooter models are Voi, Bolt, Tier, Lime, and Bird.

BOATS AND FERRIES

The Swedes are a boating people and love spending time on the water. There are almost a million leisure boats registered in the country. In Stockholm, water taxis and ferries run through the city waterways and out to the archipelago.

Stockholm is a popular stopover on international Baltic capital cruises, and it is not unusual to see gigantic cruise ships moored in the harbor towering over the colorful buildings of the Old Town.

Regular car ferries and cruise liners connect Stockholm to Helsinki and Åbo in Finland, as well as Tallinn in Estonia and Riga in Latvia. A popular Swedish pastime is to take a weekend cruise across the Baltic, enjoying the entertainment on board. Some of the ships only go as far as the Finnish island of Åland and then turn around, so passengers never disembark. The excursion enables the Swedes to purchase duty-free goods. These so-called "booze-cruises" are notorious party machines. Tickets can be bought at www.vikingline.se and www.tallinksilja.se.

There are also car ferries from Ystad in the south of Sweden to the Danish island of Bornholm;

Sightseeing by boat in the port of Helsingborg in southwestern Sweden.

from Helsingborg to Helsingör in Denmark; from Gothenburg on the west coast to either Fredrikshavn in Denmark, or to Kiel, Germany; and from Trelleborg to Rostock in Germany and Świnoujście in Poland.

WHERE TO STAY

Because demand outstrips supply, and also because of Sweden's high sales tax, staying in Sweden is usually perceived to be expensive. In fact, it does not have to be.

Hotels

The standard of hotels and hostels in Sweden is generally high, regardless of the price range. Common Web sites and apps such as Hotels.com, Booking.com, and Tripadvisor are the best way to find hotels and

The handcarved Art Suite in the Ice Hotel at Jukkasjärvi near Kiruna.

QUIRKY BOUTIQUE HOTELS IN SWEDEN

- Fabriken Furillen hotel on the island of Gotland is housed in a very dramatic former limestone factory. Beside the hotel rooms here, there are two "hermit cabins" for guests seeking isolation in nature: www.furillen.com.

- The Ice Hotel—124 miles (200 km) north of the Arctic Circle—is rebuilt each year. The Ice Hotel is a hotel and an art exhibition with ever-changing art made from ice and snow. Made completely out of natural ice from the Torne River, you drink vodka in ice glasses, and sleep on reindeer skins on blocks of ice: www.icehotel.se.

- Kolarbyn Ecolodge in Skinnskatteberg is called Sweden's most primitive hotel. It is a natural refuge for those seeking silence and adventure in a forest setting a few hours from Stockholm. Kolarbyn consists of twelve forest huts in a glade by Lake Skärsjön: www.kolarbyn.se.

- Hotel Rival in Stockholm is an old theater turned into a hip, vibrant hotel, restaurant, and lounge bar. Owned by former Abba member Benny Andersson, the theater salon still exists and hosts many events and concerts throughout the year: www.rival.se.

- The Sala Silver mine in Sala has the world's deepest hotel suite, 509 feet (155 meters) below the surface. Located in a cavernous silver mine, you are all alone, apart from the staff members above ground who are available by intercom radio: www.salasilvermine.com.

- The Steam Hotel in Västerås is a stunning modern design spa hotel built in a former steam power plant: www.steamhotel.se.

- The Tree Hotel in Harads in Lapland consists of seven tree houses, accessed by stairs, escalator, or ramps. Each tree house is completely different in design and shape, but they are all created with ecological values and in harmony with nature: www.treehotel.se.

- The Utter Inn in Västerås, 60 minutes from Stockholm is a one-of-a-kind underwater hotel, which floats on Lake Mälaren. The underwater bedroom has panorama windows in all four directions—9.8 feet (3 meters) below the surface of the water. www.utterinn.se.

secure a deal. Trusted Scandinavian hotel chains are Scandic, Radisson, and Clarion. Dedicated apps such as Airbnb help private people rent out accommodation, although this is sometimes clandestine as it is not always permitted by the housing association or tenants' board.

In recent years, there has been a major trend for quirky destination hotels in Sweden. These hotels are popular with tourists as well as with Swedes wanting an unusual staycation.

Hostels

Hostels, called *vandrahem* in Swedish, offer visitors a cheaper accommodation option. Standards differ, from budget self-catering to hotel standard, but usually they are perfectly acceptable. There are approximately 350 hostels in Sweden: www.svenskaturistforeningen.se.

The "Dragonfly," part of the Harads tree-hotel complex, is accessed by a long ramp.

Bed and Breakfast

B&Bs are another affordable option in Sweden. Check out www.bookings.com to see what is available.

Camping and Caravanning

Camping in Sweden is about experiencing nature in an unspoiled region of Europe. The National Swedish Campsite Association has more than 450 campsites where you can put up a tent or bring your caravan or motorhome. In fact, pitching a tent is allowed almost anywhere (apart from private gardens and cultivated fields) if you are there for less than twenty-four hours. More than that, and you must ask permission from the landowner. This means you can enjoy a night under the midnight sun in Swedish Lapland, or camp in a pine forest or beside countless lakes or beaches anywhere in the country. The peak season for camping in Sweden is June and July, and most of the country enjoys around twenty hours of daylight in the summer months.

SCR Swedish Camping Information

The National Swedish Campsite Association offers more than 75,000 camping pitches and 9,000 cottages and cabins. For discounts and offers related to camping, use the Camping Key Europe app or go to the Web site www.campingkeyeurope.se. The app offers discounts on ferries and includes insurance. Some Swedish campsites also accept Camping Card International, CCI.

HEALTH AND SECURITY

Health

Sweden has a state-funded medical service, although some people also take out private healthcare insurance to shorten their waiting time. Visitors can seek medical treatment at any of the public facilities. If you are from a country inside the EU or EEA, you can access healthcare in Sweden using your European Health Insurance Card (EHIC). Tourists from outside the EU/EEA do not have an automatic right to free or reduced-cost healthcare. This means you will need to show proof of insurance from your home country or comprehensive travel insurance.

If you should fall ill, www.1177.se offers free general medical advice and will refer you to specific healthcare services. You can also call 1177 for non-urgent healthcare issues. The number works nationwide, 24/7. Operators will answer questions about illness or healthcare and provide information to help you find the nearest clinic. If you are calling from abroad, or from a foreign cell phone in Sweden, call +46 771 1177 00. For non-urgent treatment, there are neighborhood clinics called Vårdcentral. It is best to call and book an appointment for these, although some clinics also have drop-in time slots. Your hotel should be able to advise.

For dental emergencies, check with your hotel reception for the nearest dental practice.

In case of medical emergency, call 112. If you are taken to hospital, you will be taken to the emergency room—*Akuten* or *Akutmottagningen* in Swedish.

Swedish hospitals are modern and clean, and all the staff speak English, as well as other languages.

For Swedish residents under twenty-five and over eighty-five a doctor's visit is free. Other age groups pay 150 SEK of the actual cost of around 2,000 SEK, with the balance being government funded.

The pioneering branch of digital healthcare known as "healthtec" is dominated by Swedish startups. This provides access to different forms of healthcare through mobiles, artificial intelligence (AI), and other technologies. Apps enable doctors and psychologists to meet patients on video links, which is popular among Swedes but not entirely without controversy. Healthtec apps also exist for veterinary visits.

Prescription medicines are available from one of the many pharmacies. Residents pay up to a maximum of 2,350 SEK per year, after which medicine is free. Until 2009, pharmacies were run by a state-owned monopoly called Apoteket, but today there are many private actors competing for the consumer.

Safety

Sweden is one of the safest countries in the world, but you should still be vigilant in built-up areas, especially at night. Pickpockets are also active in tourist-dense areas during the summer months.

The emergency number for police, fire, and ambulance is 112. Operators can speak English.

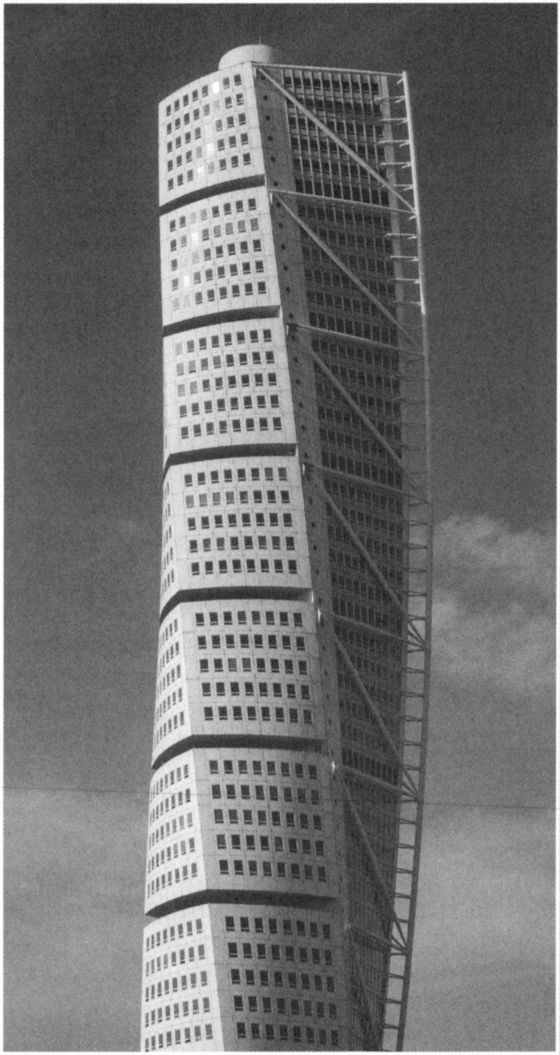

CHAPTER EIGHT

BUSINESS BRIEFING

THE BUSINESS ENVIRONMENT

Home to many successful companies with global reach, Sweden's corporate landscape includes century-old industrial companies, IT and Tech specialists, and innovative start-ups. Two-thirds of Sweden's GDP is produced in the public sector from health, transportation, and educational services—making them collectively the largest employer in the country. Sweden's open economy fosters competition and innovation, with the government proactively investing in sustainable energy companies and the biotechnology industry. Thanks to the country's educational system, the Swedish work force is highly skilled and well educated. They are also strongly protected by comprehensive labor laws, which leads to a high level of security, trust, and loyalty.

The Swedish workplace today is very multicultural and consequently many firms use English as their official company language. Swedish companies are very keen to attract talent from abroad—a necessity for survival in a small country of 10.4 million people. Having many non-Swedes in the workplace contributes to innovation and critical thinking, but can also bring misunderstandings and frustration. Some foreigners eventually adapt and learn to enjoy Swedish work culture; others find it too difficult and return to their home countries after a year or two.

WHAT MOTIVATES THE SWEDES?

Of course, money is a motivator for most Swedish people—up to a limit. Swedes also look for employers with ethical trading practices and a sense of social responsibility, who can offer them autonomy, freedom, interesting assignments, fun activities, and a good work–life balance. The average salary in Sweden is lower than salaries in Denmark and Norway (and the USA and the UK) but on a par with Finland. Sweden has a progressive income tax policy, meaning that high earners pay more tax than low earners. Tax rates vary from 32 percent to 57 percent. About 25 percent of this money goes to funding healthcare and education, and 40 percent finances the social security system.

Part of being an attractive employer in Sweden means providing internal entertainment for the personnel. It is not uncommon for employees to be treated to summer parties, lavish Christmas events, conferences in Sweden or overseas, kick-offs, and afterwork events. If alcohol is involved, the employer usually pays for one or two glasses, after which the employees buy their own. Employers in the public sector do not usually pay for alcohol consumption as the spending of taxpayers' money on such frivolity is generally frowned upon.

Reward and Recognition

Traditionally, Swedish companies have avoided rewarding and praising individuals, preferring to focus on group achievements instead. Today this has changed somewhat, and employers try to find a balance between praising the team and individual contributions. "Employee of the Month," which is found in other countries, however, is rare, and recognition is usually carried out in an informal way during a coffee break or meeting. Financial bonuses to the individual are still given in private, however, to avoid embarrassment and envy.

THE INFORMAL OFFICE

Flat hierarchy is the name of the game in most Swedish companies. This is evident in, for example, the way people dress informally, decision-making is transparent, management is accessible, and people are on first-name terms with senior staff members. A few professionals, such as lawyers and bankers, wear suits, but in general most Swedish men come to work in casual clothes such as jeans, sweaters, and shirts without a tie. Women usually wear jeans and a top, or a simple skirt or dress. Styles differ depending on the individual and the sector they work in, with the design, fashion, and advertising industries usually topping the chart for trendiness.

Many offices are open-plan, which tends to make communication less formal and easier. Managers usually sit in the open landscape with their staff, but may have their own office space for private conversations.

Functional *Fika*

Coffee time, or *fika*, is very important in Swedish culture and this extends to the workplace. By law, Swedes are entitled to two fifteen-minute coffee breaks, one in the morning and one in the afternoon. The purpose of these breaks is to provide an organized opportunity for socializing and networking with colleagues and the boss. *Fika* is an informal event, but there is also an unspoken obligation to attend. If an office celebrates someone's birthday, it is during the coffee break and the birthday boy or girl usually brings in a cake to share.

OFFICE HOURS AND AVAILABILITY

The office working week is Monday through Friday from 8.00 or 9:00 a.m. until 5:00 or 6:00 p.m., although most people are available for contact outside these hours. Lunch is usually thirty minutes, and there are the two daily coffee breaks. Lunch can start as early as 11:00 a.m. but is usually over by 2:00 p.m.

The working week is forty hours. Overtime can only be requested in exceptional circumstances, but flextime is common. This is a great help, as many Swedish parents choose to arrive early at work so that they can leave early to pick up their children from kindergarten, and it is not unusual for offices to start emptying out at 3:00 p.m. Many Swedes then make up their lost hours at home later in the evening once the children have been put to bed.

If an employee is sick, they get no pay for the first day, and then they receive statutory sick pay from their employer for two weeks. At day fifteen, they receive sickness benefit from the government. The employer has the right to demand a doctor's note, usually after seven days off. Paid time off is also an entitlement if a parent or guardian has to stay home to care for a sick child. In Swedish staying home for this reason is called *vabbing*.

Due to the high level of trust in Sweden, many employers allow their staff to work from home. During the coronavirus pandemic that began in March 2020, everybody who could work from home was instructed to do so, with some offices completely closing into 2021. About 50 percent of the working population regularly work from home.

Holidays

Swedish workers, by law, get twenty-five days (five weeks) paid vacation days a year. Many people take several consecutive weeks between midsummer in June through the second week in August. In fact, most employees have a legal right to four weeks consecutive vacation, unless they belong to certain professional categories or it is specified differently in their contracts. This often means that offices are running on a skeleton staff during the summer period, which can affect projects, deadlines, and customer service. This lack of availability can sometimes be hard to understand for overseas customers and colleagues.

UNIONS

The first labor union was started in 1880, and today approximately 70 percent of Swedish workers belong to one. Historically, the unions have done much to improve the working conditions of their members. Today, the unions regulate essential parts of the Swedish labor market, such as wage levels, holidays, and pensions. As members of a union, Swedes have a strong safety net, protection in disputes, representation at the negotiating table, and support and advice. Joining a union is also a way to secure an income in the event of unemployment as all unions have unemployment funds (*a-kassor*) and special income insurances.

GENDER REPRESENTATION

In Sweden, about 66 percent of all women and 70 percent of all men are in work, although around 30 percent of the women are employed part-time. Membership of the Swedish parliament is equally distributed between the sexes, with almost half of the members being female. This is higher than the EU average of around one-third. In the upper echelons of the business world, however, the picture looks somewhat different. Here, only 16 percent of managing directors and CEOs are female. Like many countries, Sweden also struggles with a gender pay gap, with women earning on average 12 percent less than their male counterparts in the same role. Sweden has come far regarding gender equality in the workplace and society, but still has a way to go.

Working remotely over breakfast in a coffee shop.

The "Me Too" movement of 2017 hit hard in Sweden, as in many places around the world, with cases of sexual harassment and abuse being reported in all types of workplaces. A major part of the debate in Sweden focused on the affair surrounding an author whose wife sat in the Swedish Academy, the high-profile organization that awards the annual Nobel Prize for Literature. The author was accused by eighteen women of sexual assault and harassment. The scandal led to several members of the Swedish Academy resigning and the organization's credibility was indelibly damaged.

THE MANAGER AS COACH

Given the Swedish values of equality and self-sufficiency, it is not surprising that a specific kind of management has arisen in Sweden. The Swedes like to see their managers as coaches or facilitators. Managers uphold openness and two-way communication, rather than take an authoritarian approach. Swedish managers and staff prefer to make decisions together, to reach a workable consensus. It is considered important that everybody be included in the process and listened to. This can take time and be frustrating for anyone wanting a quick decision and speedy implementation. Information tends to flow well between management and staff and through the organization, and employees are given enough responsibility to complete their tasks without too much unnecessary management involvement.

This style of management may be perceived as weak or submissive by foreigners, but most Swedes would argue that their democratic approach contributes strongly to job motivation and work–life balance.

Defining Consensus

The concept of consensus is defined differently in different cultures. In the English-speaking world, it tends to mean that everybody agrees with each other. To a Swede, consensus means that everybody has an opportunity to give their opinion, issues are discussed in a fair way, and that everybody can agree to live with the decision that is made. You might not actually be in agreement, but you agree to implement whatever decision the group has arrived at. Understanding this is key to understanding certain attitudes or forms of behavior you may encounter at long, drawn out meetings.

TEAMWORK

Sweden has a strong tradition of teamwork—the expression "*ensam är inte stark*" (literally, alone is not strong) being a kind of mantra. Over a century ago, when Sweden was largely an agrarian society, it was nearly impossible to survive long-term on your own—you needed the group to help with many farming and harvest tasks. Today, we see this reflected in, for example, cleaning days when neighbors get together and collectively clean their communal spaces, or in boat clubs where people gather to help each other put the boats into or take them out of the water. During the Viking era, the most severe punishment was to become *fredlös*—banished from the community and outside the protection of the law. Today, in Swedish workplaces we see a strong emphasis on inclusion and representation, so that nobody feels excluded and unwelcome, and teamwork is highly prioritized.

In the Swedish education system, group work is often more highly valued than individual achievement. Swedes learn from an early age to work together to solve problems. In school, they are placed in teams to tackle an assignment and arrive at a group analysis. The strongest are taught to help the weakest.

In the workplace, Swedish companies easily adapt work efficiency models such as Tuckman and AGILE. Focusing on team dynamics, the most popular leadership training program in Sweden is called UGL— "Understanding the Group and Leader." Developed for the Swedish National Defense Academy in the 1980s, and based on Susan Wheelen's research on the dynamics of work teams, it is by far the most attended leadership development course in Sweden.

SETTING UP A MEETING

Making a phone call or sending an e-mail is the best way to try to make contact. Don't be surprised if you do not get an answer, however, as most people do not feel obliged to reply. LinkedIn is a popular way of contacting people and for job seeking. If applying for a job, it is usually acceptable to write in English. Include a cover letter with your CV and emphasise your strengths, but avoid bragging or making empty claims.

Get the Timing Right

When setting up a meeting, be aware that Swedish businesses use week numbers to define time—January 1 being in Week 1, and December 31 being in Week 52. If you are conducting business that is time-sensitive, you should also be aware of the public holidays in Sweden, many of which fall in the spring and early summer. Finalizing an agreement from the end of June (Week 25) to the beginning of August (Week 37) can be difficult, as well as during the festive season from the week before Christmas (Week 51) to after January 13 (Week 3).

When writing, Swedes use the 24-hour clock to describe time, so 3:00 p.m. is 1500 hours. Appointments are made in advance, and punctuality is regarded as respectful and therefore extremely important. This applies to face-to-face meetings as well as virtual ones. It is equally important to end the meeting on time, as many Swedes have packed schedules. For this reason, many meetings are booked for 50 minutes to allow a breather before the next meeting starts. When wrapping up a meeting, remember to summarize the action points and even confirm them in an e-mail afterward.

MAKING A PRESENTATION

A typical Swedish presentation is efficient and factual. Whatever the level of detail and length of speech required—technical presentations, for example, tend to be detailed and complex and therefore longer—Swedes prefer to get to the point quickly.

A Swedish audience is usually attentive. They will listen intently and not interrupt the speaker. Questions will come at the end of the presentation or on other occasions when the presenter elicits them. The audience is unlikely to communicate their engagement actively. Their body language may be still and their expressions impassive, which can disturbing for foreign presenters, who may think that they are not interested or do not understand.

The Swedes appreciate logical argumentation and are suspicious of a "manipulative" hard sell. Humor is welcomed as it lightens the mood, although from a cultural perspective this can be risky. For example, self-deprecating humor can be perceived as unprofessional and unserious. Swedish audiences generally like visual aids, so informative slides are welcome.

NEGOTIATIONS

Meetings and negotiations are generally well-structured and time-conscious. The agenda will usually be sent in advance. Small talk in Sweden (tellingly referred to as "cold talk") usually only lasts a few minutes before people get down to business. The Swedes see negotiations as a joint problem-solving process rather than a competition. This means that they will aim for a win/win rather than win/lose resolution. Very little emotion is expressed during negotiations and propositions are most persuasive if they are backed up with evidence. It is strongly advisable to avoid open confrontation or conflict and to remain calm, friendly, patient, and persistent. The Swedish negotiating style is straightforward, unaggressive, and honest and they dislike negotiators who use negative tactics such as telling lies, giving false information, or applying pressure.

Swedish negotiators believe in information sharing as a way of building trust, even though they may not so readily reveal everything on their part. They do not appreciate an aggressive sales pitch, and generally dislike bargaining and haggling. A Swede will often start with an "already-fair" asking price and will not expect to move too far from it. It would be unusual and unnecessary for a Swedish company to bring in a lawyer at the initial phase, which could be seen as a sign of mistrust.

After a negotiation it is common practice to e-mail a thank you and/or a summary of the agreements reached and next steps to be taken.

CONTRACTS

Verbal agreements are considered binding in Sweden, although they are always written up subsequently as contracts. Swedish civil law, especially purchase and contract law, covers most possible situations, and a Swedish contract will therefore not be as specific or as long as a contract based on British common law. The written contract will usually include detailed terms and conditions, and it is recommended you consult a local legal expert before signing.

Swedish contracts are almost always dependable. Disputes between different service providers or between service providers and consumers are tried in district courts. The summons application is normally filed at the district court in the city where the counter party, called the respondent, is resident, unless otherwise specified in the contract.

MANAGING DISAGREEMENT

Because of their tendency to seek consensus and their strong belief in maintaining harmony, Swedish people are generally open, friendly, and polite. Disputes, if they happen at all, will be couched in factual and clear language, with little open expression of hostility or emotion. Many Swedes are suspicious of displays of negative emotion in the workplace, as it does not seem appropriate or mature. This lack of expressiveness can lead foreigners to perceive Swedes as unfeeling, cold or, even worse, arrogant. But rest assured, the feelings are there, even if they are not overtly expressed.

Fear of Conflict

One stereotypical view of the Swedes is that they are afraid of conflict, and this might very well be the case with some individuals. A Swede may be less inclined to pick a fight or tell a stranger off than other people around the world. However, in a country that prioritizes harmony, looks for consensus, and focuses on inclusion and discussion, it is easy to see why the need for conflict is reduced. It might simply be that Swedes are more likely to agree with each other and more willing to compromise, than enter a confrontation.

WORKING IN SWEDEN

EU citizens are entitled to work in Sweden without a work permit. Generally, citizens from countries outside the EU must apply for a work permit through the Swedish Migration Agency. Once you can work, make sure to register with the Tax Office to receive a Swedish personal identification number. This number is the key to accessing the Swedish system.

All employees have a work contract. One to three months' notice of termination is required of both parties to end it. Most jobs start with a probation period of six months during which employment can be terminated at any point. After six months, employment becomes permanent and is much more secure. If a company must lay off staff, the "last-in, first-out" principle applies in most cases although there are a few exceptions.

Other less secure forms of employment are project-specific employment and temporary employment for a given period, or to replace people on parental leave or long-term sickness. Go to www.arbetsformedling.se for more details about the specific forms of employment and your rights as an employee.

STARTING A BUSINESS

Certain types of businesses in Sweden require a permit to operate. For detailed information, go to www. verksamt.se.

If you want to operate as a sole trader, your company will carry the same number as your personal number. To start up, you apply for F-skatt (Entrepreneur Tax) to declare that you will not be working as an employee for a company, but you will be working for yourself. For more information, check out the Swedish Tax Office at www.skatteverket.se.

Citizens of the EU/EEA are also entitled to residence in Sweden without registering with the Swedish Migration Agency and can apply for a personal identity number. Citizens from outside the EU/EEA/Switzerland who intend to start a business, must apply for a residence permit before coming to Sweden.

For business entry support, go to www.business. sweden.com and www.vinnova.se. For more information

on starting or running a business in Sweden, go to
www.workinginsweden.se.

The Cost of Business

The highest costs for most companies are the costs of
premises and personnel. Companies pay an employer
tax on top of most employee's wages—set in 2021 at
31.42 percent of gross salary. This makes employing
staff rather expensive and is constantly being debated
between the political parties. Corporate tax on profits
was set at an internationally competitive rate of
20.6 percent in 2021.

BUSINESS ENTERTAINMENT

Taking a customer or business partner out to eat
is common in Sweden, but inviting them home
is unusual. At lunch, people usually refrain from
drinking alcohol but at dinner they may drink
moderately. Around Christmas time, it is popular to
invite people to a Christmas *julbord* to celebrate the
festive season. Some companies, however, have strict
anti-corruption policies and do not allow their staff to
accept invitations for lunch or dinner from suppliers.
This may even extend to the receiving of gifts,
however small.

CHAPTER NINE

COMMUNICATING

LANGUAGE

A branch of the Indo-European family of languages, Swedish is Teutonic in origin. Most Norwegians, Danes, and Swedes understand each other, although spoken Danish is the hardest for Swedes to comprehend.

Up until 1809, Finland was a part of Sweden. As a legacy of this, Swedish is still considered a national language of Finland and is a mandatory subject for Finnish-speaking pupils in the last four years of primary school (grades 6 to 9). Some of the 90 percent of Finnish citizens who are native Finnish speakers strongly object to this, calling it "enforced Swedish" and a form of cultural colonialism. Approximately 5 percent of Finland's population regard Swedish as their mother tongue.

The level of spoken English in Sweden is high, thanks to the Swedish education system, the media, and the Internet. A brand of English, and a source of humor, called "Swenglish" (*Svengelska*) has emerged, where the two languages are playfully mixed to create texture in a conversation.

Swedish has a smaller vocabulary than English, so when a Swede speaks English it can sound literal and rather brusque. Do not be offended if you encounter this—it is simply a reflection of the direct and economical style of Swedish speech.

COMMUNICATION STYLES

The Swedish communication style is brief and straightforward in comparison to English. Whereas English uses a lot of euphemisms and contextual reference, the meaning of Swedish is usually in the words

themselves. What is said is what is meant, and there is very little need to read between the lines. For example, if a Swede says "I will try my best" it generally means exactly that. They will do everything in their power to do their best. In contrast, if an English-speaking person says this it can mean that they will do it if they get round to it. Swedes say what they mean, and for them it is a question of honor and integrity. One exception to this directness is where there is a potential confrontation, in which case the Swedish language tends to become more contextual and indirect in order to preserve harmony.

Introductions

If a Swede does not introduce you to another person, do not take offense. You are expected to take responsibility for introducing yourself with a handshake, direct eye contact, and your name. In informal situations it is enough to give only your first name. Business meetings will usually begin with everybody introducing themselves.

HUMOR

Given the international stereotype of being cool and serious, it is no surprise that Swedes are not known for their sense of humor. The truth is, however, that they are very funny—once you are on their wavelength.

Swedish humor falls into two camps: the understated and the slapstick. On the one hand, it can be very dry, ironic, and dark, which does not always translate easily to people from other cultures. What makes a Swede laugh may leave foreigners totally confused and uncomprehending. Swedes often love awkward humor, with the hit TV series "Solsidan" and the English series "The Office" leading the way in this category.

On the other hand, there is broad slapstick, with funny voices, silly walks, falling over, and cross-dressing. This kind of entertainment is popular in theaters, and the leading Swedish comedian Robert Gustavsson is a prime example. Yet another type of humor is the pun—particularly popular on the west coast of Sweden. It is so associated with this region that it is referred to as the "Gothenburg pun." These jokes make you laugh and groan in equal measure.

A Gothenburg Pun

How much space was freed up when Britain left the EU?
1GB

American and British comedy shows are very popular in Sweden, with classics such as "Seinfeld," "Friends," "Absolutely Fabulous," and "The Big Bang Theory" being frequently referenced.

In the business world Swedes will almost always be friendly, but will probably not crack jokes in order to help build relationships or smooth things over. To Brits and Americans this can seem distant or stand-offish, but it is not intended so—it is just not the usual approach in Sweden.

SILENCE

Visitors may find that the Swedes are not very talkative. Naturally this varies, with some being very chatty and others preferring to take a back seat. For most Swedes, though, politeness involves turn-taking in conversation, which includes waiting for the other party to finish speaking, rather than interrupting them. If you are used to a more dynamic conversational style, and to being interrupted, there may be more silences than you are used to, which can feel stilted or awkward. A way to survive this is to embrace the silence, rather than fill it with unnecessary nonsense.

It may be a Jante legacy, but for many Swedes inconsequential chitchat does not come naturally and can make them uncomfortable. In recent years organized networking events—enabling people to practice the skill of small talk in a structured context—have become widespread. When making small talk with a Swede, don't ask too many personal questions, which can be regarded as inappropriate or prying. Instead, keep it neutral. The weather, the location you are in, and general questions about Sweden are three safe and easy topics.

NONVERBAL COMMUNICATION

Eye contact is an important part of Swedish communication. Most Swedes prefer prolonged direct eye contact while talking or listening, which can be unnerving if you are not used to it. In terms of body language, Swedes are generally less expressive than many other people, preferring to rely on the words themselves rather than expansive gestures or movements. This reserved style can lead to misunderstandings, with foreigners perceiving them as insensitive or cold. When speaking, they usually keep the voice low to moderate—screaming or shouting is regarded as immature and unprofessional in a workplace. When a Swede listens, he or she may nod their head and say "mm." This means they are listening, and not necessarily that they agree.

THE MEDIA

Freedom of speech is protected by law and no form of media is subject to censorship. There are, however, restrictions regarding child pornography and libel. Swedish law also prohibits hate speech against ethnic or other groups regarding their race, skin color, national or ethnic origin, sexual orientation, or religion.

In 1991, the Swedish parliament added the Fundamental Law on Freedom of Expression to the Swedish Constitution. This addition bans incitement to violence against ethnic minorities in the audio-visual media, including radio, television, film and, to a certain extent, the Internet.

Public-Service Broadcasting
Since 1956, Sweden has had a state-owned television and radio service called SVT, for which every tax-paying adult pays a licensing fee that is deducted from their tax returns. The maximum yearly fee was 1,347 SEK in 2020. In return, SVT provides two main channels as well as an educational channel, a news channel, a channel for children, and a streaming site called SVT Play. There are also several public-service radio channels.

Commercial Channels
Sweden was one of the first countries in the world to launch digital terrestrial television, in April 1999, which caused the number of television channels to multiply. TV4 is the largest and most popular of the commercial channels. Streaming services such as Netflix, HBO, Amazon Prime, and C-more as well as YouTube compete with the scheduled television channels.

The Press
All publications in Sweden are offered as online subscriptions. A few national broadsheets can still be bought in print form, such as *Dagens Nyheter* and *Svenskadagbladet*, as well as the tabloid papers *Aftonbladet* and *Expressen*. Many magazines also still come out in print, with gossip magazines such as *HäntExtra*, and *Svenskdamtidning* being among the

most popular. Crossword magazines are also common. Online subscription service www.readly.se gathers all the common magazines in English and Swedish together on one accessible platform.

Between 2011 and 2018 Sweden became the first country in the world to hand over its official Twitter account, @sweden, to its citizens and let a new person tweet as @sweden every week. The idea was to showcase Sweden's diversity and freedom of expression.

TELEPHONES

The fixed-line telephone is truly a dinosaur in Sweden, with only 1 percent of the population owning a subscription. Everything is mobile, and 98 percent of households have access to broadband. There are no telephone booths—the last one was removed in 2015. The country code for Sweden is 46, followed by a city code and the telephone number. To dial outside Sweden, put 00 before the relevant country code. The 112 toll-free number for medical emergencies can also be used for police, fire, or ambulance services, and the operators speak English.

To find phone numbers and addresses, www.hitta. se and www.eniro.se are useful sites. Search engines for finding services around your immediate location are www.yelp.com and www.google.se.

Due to the fast broadband and Wi-Fi services in Sweden, free VoIP services such as Skype, Facetime, and WhatsApp work exceedingly well. If you are calling a Swede, expect them to answer the phone with their name or maybe a "*Hej!*" When finishing a call, they will say, "*Hej*," "*Hej då*," or even a cheerful "*Hej, hej*." Avoid calling after 10:00 p.m.

MAJOR CITY CODES	
Stockholm (0)8	Gothenburg (0)31
Malmö (0)40	Uppsala (0)18

THE INTERNET

Most cafés offer free Wi-Fi; just ask at the counter for the password when you order your coffee. There are also a lot of public Wi-Fi hotspots at, for example, airports, stations, public squares, and libraries.

The Online Generation
Given that such a large proportion of Swedes are connected, it comes as no surprise that the smartphone has changed the way in which people live their lives. Socializing, dating, shopping, entertainment, and healthcare are all available via digital devices. However, according to official statistics, almost 10 percent of the Swedish population say that they have never or almost never used the Internet. This group is made up of people born outside Europe, people in low-income

households, and the elderly. As the majority of Swedes enjoy ever more digital flexibility and convenience, this 10 percent become increasingly isolated. For younger Swedes, smart devices are a matter of course and totally natural.

One impact of digitalization in Sweden is the blurring of what is considered public information and what is private. Traditionally, there was a clear boundary between the two realms. However, the younger generations tend to be very open and personal on social media—behavior that the older generation does not always appreciate.

MAIL

The Swedish postal system is run by PostNord and is rather decentralized. Stamps and envelopes can be bought at PostNord postal service points and also at grocery stores and the convenience-store chains Pressbyrån and 7-Eleven. For postage rates, go to www.postnord.se.

To post a letter or postcard, drop them into a yellow mailbox. For larger packages, you must go to a PostNord service point, although some local supermarkets, convenience stores, gas stations, and other similar shops also offer this service. When you order something online, you normally select where you would like the parcel to be delivered for collection. When it arrives, you will receive a notification via e-mail or SMS confirming this. You'll need to bring this notification and your personal ID with you when collecting it. If you are collecting on behalf of somebody else, you'll need to show their ID card.

CONCLUSION

The Swedes strike a delicate balance between preserving their traditions and welcoming the new. As a society, they strive to be the most progressive in the world—a place of civility, equality, solidarity, and with a high quality of life. This is, of course, a work in progress, but, looking with outside eyes, one can appreciate the huge advances they have made. The country has its challenges; however, by holding to the enduring values of honesty, sincerity, and mutual trust, the Swedes are well-positioned to deal with whatever comes their way.

The Swedes live in exceptional harmony with their environment, and Sweden is a fascinating mixture of clean urban areas and breathtaking natural beauty. For the visitor, the dramatic and varied landscape—from Arctic mountains to dense forests and wonderful lakes and waterways—can be a magical discovery. Sweden's cities combine history and tradition with a thoroughly modern urban experience, with trendy restaurants, great shopping, and a vibrant nightlife. Whatever direction your travels take you, you will be blown away by this beautiful, civilized country in the North and its friendly, sophisticated, and outward-looking people.

APPENDIX 1: SWEDISH SPORTING LEGENDS

Despite having a small population, Sweden has produced many sporting legends:

Annika Sörenstam—professional golfer, regarded as one of the best golfers ever, winner of 90 international tournaments.

Armand Duplantis—eneregtic pole vaulter and the 2020 world record holder at 20.275 feet/6.18 meters.

Björn Borg—cool tennis player who became the first man to win 11 Grand Slam singles titles.

Börje Salming—ice hockey player with idol status, named one of the "100 Greatest NHL Players" in history.

Ingemar Stenmark—alpine skiier who has more international races than any other alpine skier to date.

Sara Sjöström—impressive swimmer and current world record holder in four different swimming categories. Has won 16 individual medals at World Championships, more than any other female swimmer in history.

Zlatan Ibrohimoviz—one of the most decorated football strikers of his generation with 31 trophies so far.

APPENDIX 2: USEFUL APPS

Travel and Transportation
SAS – Scandinavian Airlines – Sweden's largest provider of international and domestic flights.
Flygresor – search engine for flights.
Momondo – search engine flights and accommodation.
SL – tickets and timetables for local transportation in Stockholm.
SJ – train tickets and timetables for whole of Sweden.
TaxiStockholm – taxi booking service in Stockholm.
Taxi Goteborg – taxi booking service in Gothenburg.
Bolt – taxi service.
Uber – taxi service.
Voi – electric scooter booking and payment.
Tier – electric scooter booking and payment.

Communication

WhatsApp – messaging and call service.

Skype – messaging and call service.

Zoom – meeting and call service.

Viber – messaging and call service.

Hitta – for finding addresses and telephone numbers.

Shopping and Food

Karma – app which locates reduced price restaurant food that would otherwise be discarded.

Foodora – for ordering home delivery restaurant food from a variety of restaurants.

Wolt – for ordering home delivery restaurant food from a variety of restaurants.

Uber Eats – for home delivery restaurant food.

Max Express – ordering service of food and drink from Sweden's popular equivalent to McDonald's.

Systembolaget – information on alcohol available in Sweden. Alcohol cannot be ordered via the app. This can only be done on www.systembolaget.se or in one of the Systembolaget stores.

The Fork – find and book a table at a restaurant.

Bokabord – find and book a table at a restaurant.

APPENDIX 3: USEFUL WEB SITES

www.sweden.se (information about Sweden)

www.visitsweden.com

www.visitstockholm.se

www.watchingtheswedes.se (blog about Swedish life and culture)

www.newbieguidetosweden.se (guide to Sweden for new arrivals)

www.thelocal.se (local news in English)

FURTHER READING

Anderson, Bengt. *Swedishness.* Stockholm: Positiva Sverige, 1993, 1995/ Sandberg Trygg, 2000.

Åsbrink, Elisabeth. *Made in Sweden—25 ideas that created a country.* London: Faber and Faber, 2019.

Booth, Michael. *The Almost Nearly Perfect People.* London: Jonathan Cape, 2014.

Bourelle, Julien S. *The Swedes, a happy culture of Scandinavia.* Drammen: Mondå, 2018.

Britton, Claes. *Sweden and the Swedes.* Stockholm: The Swedish Institute, 2001.

Brown, Andrew. *Fishing in Utopia: Sweden and the future that disappeared.* London: Granta Books, 2009.

Downman, Lorna, Paul Britten Austin and Anthony Baird. *Round the Swedish Year: Daily Life And Festivals Through Four Seasons.* Stockholm: Bokförlaget Fabel, 1972 (digitized 2009).

Dunne, Linnea. *Lagom: The Swedish Art of Balanced Living.* London: Octopus, 2017.

Hadenius, Stig. *Swedish Politics During the 20th Century.* Stockholm: The Swedish Institute, 1999.

Magnusson, Margareta. *The Gentle Art of Swedish Death Cleaning.* New York: Scribner, 2018.

Moon, Colin. *Sweden: The Secret Files. What They'd Rather Keep to Themselves.* Uppsala, Sweden: Today Press AB/Colin Moon Communications AB, 2002.

Robinowitz, Christina Johansson and Lisa Werner Carr. *Modern-Day Vikings. A Practical Guide to Interacting with the Swedes.* Boston and London: Intercultural Press, 2001.

Rossel, Sven H. and Bo Elbrond-Bek (eds.) (transl. David W. Colbert). *Christmas in Scandinavia.* Lincoln, Nebraska, and London: University of Nebraska, 1999.

Sandell, Kaj. *Eyewitness Travel Guides Stockholm.* London: Dorling Kindersley Ltd., 2001.

Swahn, Jan-Öjvind (transl. Roger Tanner). *Maypoles, Crayfish and Lucia: Swedish Holidays and Traditions.* Värnamo, Sweden: The Swedish Institute, 1997.

PICTURE CREDITS

INDEX

Acknowledgment

With thanks to Charlotte DeWitt, author of the first edition of *Culture Smart! Sweden*, for her many insights into Swedish culture.